DRIVE ON

"Special Magic" and *"Special Moment,"* pair of Hackney ponies driven to a Physicians Phaeton. Owned and driven by the author, Doris L. Ganton.

DRIVE ON

Training and Showing the Advanced Driving Horse

Doris L. Ganton

SOUTH BRUNSWICK AND NEW YORK: A. S. BARNES AND COMPANY
LONDON THOMAS YOSELOFF LTD

Other books by DORIS L. GANTON:
Breaking and Training the Driving Horse
Lucky—The Horse Nobody Wanted
Lucky Becomes a Star

© 1979 by A. S. Barnes and Co., Inc.

A. S. Barnes and Co., Inc.
Cranbury, New Jersey 08512

Thomas Yoseloff Ltd
Magdalen House
136-148 Tooley Street
London SE1 2TT, England

Library of Congress Cataloging in Publication Data

Ganton, Doris L   1931-
  Drive on.

  1. Show driving of horse-drawn vehicles. 2. Horse
training. I. Title. II. Title: Advanced driving horse.
III. Title: Driving horse.
SF305.7.G36   636.1′08′88   78-69658
ISBN 0-498-02255-2

PRINTED IN THE UNITED STATES OF AMERICA

To Shanfara
in recognition of his years of faithful service
in helping train thousands of aspiring "whips"
the thrill and techniques of driving. His
patience, cheerfulness, cooperation, and
charity have achieved for this fine Arabian
a fond and affectionate reputation.

Contents

Braiding
Cleaning the Harness
Grooming
Harnessing
Packing the Show Trunk

DRIVE ON

1
TRAINING

Standards

In any type of advanced work a certain level of competence is expected in order to achieve a standard from which further work can be carried on. A recommended study on the basics, incorporating the methods of achieving such a standard, is *Breaking and Training the Driving Horse* (reference 1).

The advanced training described in this book begins exactly where the previous book left off and is based on the assumption that the horse in training has received the complete instruction described within its pages.

To refresh the memory of those who are familiar with "Breaking and Training the Driving Horse" and to assist those who are not, we will outline the steps leading up to the level from which we will begin our advanced work.

Basic Training

A youngster is usually started in harness work around the age of two years. At this age, he is mentally and physically capable of receiving and understanding training techniques when presented to him in logical fashion. The colt is first taught to lunge and to obey voice commands on the lunge line, and is introduced to a bit by allowing him to carry a light snaffle in his mouth as he eats or lunges. Handling and early association with a young horse generates confidence and creates a relationship of trust and willingness which is so necessary in a training program.

When the colt is lunging well both ways of the ring, the harness may be gradually introduced. This is best done on cross ties or wherever the colt is normally tied for grooming or handling. The backpad and crupper are placed on the colt gently and tactfully and he is lunged with this amount of harness on at the walk and trot. When he has accepted this completely, an open bridle should be put on using the same snaffle bit to which he has become accustomed. The long driving lines are run through the rein terrets on the backpad and buckled to the snaffle bit. The colt is driven from the ground beginning on the lunging cirle which he understands. Gradually, the colt is steered out of the relatively small lunging circle and driven on the rail. Crossovers down the diagonal of the ring should be done frequently to achieve a change of direction and accustom the colt to being driven both ways of the ring. The driver should take up a position about three feet to the inside and to the rear of the colt for utmost control and safety, and with each crossover should change sides. The colt should be driven in circles and figure eights beginning with large ones and gradually working down to fairly small ones requiring flexion and bending. In this manner the colt becomes well balanced and obedient to the reins as well as learning the proper way to corner and turn on his haunches.

When the colt is proficient at his work in an open bridle, the blinker bridle should be put on and the preceeding work in circles and figures repeated. Now the colt's trust and confidence in his driver comes to the fore, as with most of his side and rear vision cut off he has to rely on his driver and obey commands regardless of his inability to see.

Once the colt had accepted the blinkers and can do his work well and obediently in them, the breast collar and traces are put on. A helper is needed from this point on and will make the further training safer and easier for both horse and trainer.

The "trace aids" are the first step in actual work done by our colt, and this is where our helper first comes into the picture. The traces are run through the shaft loops and tied together at their ends, while a long rope or halter shank is attached. The helper holds this long rope and walks behind the colt—at a safe distance—and exerts varying amounts of "pull" on the horses's chest via the traces. The driver is in control driving from the inside and he must give the commands to his helper regarding when and how much pressure to exert. Very light amounts are pulled at first to prepare to the colt and the driver must encourage the colt to go on. He should *never* be allowed to halt against the pull; this can lead to a balky horse in the future. As the colt learns to resist the pull and keep moving, more pressure and for longer periods is applied until the colt can pull easily and readily—even around the corners. The helper should firmly swing out from side to side a few times to get the colt used to pressure on his sides and flanks. This will prepare him for the next step, which is work in poles.

Poles are simply two freshly cut small trees about three inches in diameter and ten feet in length. They are joined back about six feet from the tips by a 2″ × 6″ board, forming a wedge shape with tips 26″ apart and distance across the crossbar about 48″. They resemble the old Indian travois design and since they are green they are resilient and difficult to break. Two small hooks are inserted at either end of the crossbar to which the traces will be attached. The tips of the poles should be whittled down until they slide freely into the shaft loops.

The poles are placed in the ring and the colt driven up to them and allowed to become familiar with their sight and smell. The helper then stands between the tips, picking them up and dragging them off as the trainer drives the colt behind as closely as he can manage. At first, this will be quite a distance away because the colt will be frightened, but eventually he will move up beside the poles and pass them. For a few days the driver should play "leap frog" with the poles—driving the colt past the poles as close as possible then halting and having the poles dragged by the colt and halted out in his sight. This will accustom the colt to the noise behind his blinkers and the sight of the poles going by, which correlated with the noise will be filed away mentally as harmless. After several days of this work, the colt should be paying little attention to the poles and will have accepted them. He is now ready to hitch in the poles, another important step in his education.

Position the poles at one end of the longest side of the ring and with a halter on under his bridle, lead him up to the front of the poles ready to have them drawn up over his croup. The helper holds the colt at his head while the trainer hitches him in the poles—a process which should be accomplished as quickly as possible. As soon as the traces are hooked on the trainer picks up the reins and with the helper leading the colt to give him confidence, drives off down the long side of the ring.

The first two corners must be rounded with great care and attention or the colt may get sideways in the poles and become frightened. The helper plays a large part in steadying him at this criticial point of his training. After a few rounds of the ring in one direction, the colt should be dirven down the diagonal and a change of direction effected. Care should be taken to make the turns large and very round to keep the poles from bumping him. A few rounds in the new direction and the trainer can begin to relax a bit. On the next series of turns he will allow the pole to touch the colt as he makes a corner, keeping enough outside rein on him to correct the situation quickly if the need arises. More and more contact with the pole can be allowed until the colt has no fear of them at all and can shove them around the corners with ease and ability. Now the helper can be dispensed with, although it is wise to have him stand in the center of the ring in case of emergency.

From now on, we will work the colt in circles and figures to teach him the proper method of handling himself in shafts and also how to cope with the shafts on corners and in tight turns. Initially, the circles and figures will be large and require little bending or shoving of the poles. But as the size decreases, the colt will have to shove the inside pole and cross his legs both front and rear to effect a proper and balanced turn.

Halts must be done often and the colt made to stand still for increasing lengths of time. This is something he will have to do in the show ring and it must be taught right from the beginning. When standing as in a lineup, he should be discouraged from attempting to back up because uncontrolled backing up can be extremely dangerous and very expensive in terms of broken equipment. The colt should not be taught or allowed to back up for at least a month after he has been driving forward in the cart. In harness, above all else, forward motion must be established.

After a week in poles, the colt usually is proficient and steady enough to be hitched in a cart. Some colts take longer than others to reach this stage, but a good trainer always knows when this point is reached. It is wiser to wait a few days longer and keep him at his work in poles than to risk damage and a possible set back in training by hitching him too soon in the cart. During the period spent in poles, the check rein on the colt can usually be shortened slightly until it is actually doing some good in its' intended use. It should not be made too tight, but rather just short enough to force the colt to carry his head in an alert position and take the weight off his forehand should he be inclined in that direction. It must not restrict the freedom of his motion nor make his action stilted; it is merely to keep his attention concentrated and to lift the front to a small degree.

A two-wheeled cart is preferable to hitch a youngster to initially. A cart can turn 360° if the colt wheels and is much easier to control. It is generally of much sturdier construction and less breakable than a four-wheeled buggy. The two-wheeled cart is very similar to the poles and its action is much the same for our colt, so the transition is not as great as it would be with another vehicle.

The cart is pulled into the ring and the colt driven up to it and allowed to smell it and become accustomed to this new object. The helper then pulls the cart around in the same manner as the poles while the driver guides the colt in the same "leap frog" procedure. This part of the training program rarely takes more than a few minutes. With his previous conditioning in the poles, the colt usually accepts the new equipment readily and ceases to show fear or shy from it in a couple of rounds of the ring.

Now we are ready to hitch in the cart. A halter is placed on the colt under his driving bridle and a safety line snapped onto it. The helper leads the colt by this safety line and will assist the trainer when necessary at the colt's head. The colt is led or driven into a position directly in front of the shafts of the cart, which is placed at one end of the longest side of the ring. The helper stands at the colt's head, keeping him quiet as the trainer quickly hitches him in the cart. The trainer drives from the ground on the inside, approximately opposite the crossbar, in the same position as when driving in poles. The helper leads the colt off as the trainer drives and gradually moves back behind the colt's blinkers out of his vision as the colt settles to his work. In the event of trouble the helper is in the proper position to control the colt and give assistance to the driver.

The colt should be driven in both directions of the ring before the driver mounts into the cart, just to be certain no problems exist. He should mount in the cart lightly and sit quietly so as not to upset the colt by a jerky movement on his back via the shafts and shaft loops. After a round or so, the safety line can be removed and the helper remain in the center of the ring.

The first few lessons in the cart should be done at the walk, and will be a repeat of the work in poles with circles, figures and halts. As the colt becomes proficient and adept at the walk, he should be encouraged to jog for very short distances until he becomes used to the up and down motion created by the shafts. He can then be asked to move on at a trot and to manage the circles and figures at this greater speed. He will have to learn to balance on his corners while bending into them which is more difficult for him now that he is actually hitched to a cart.

From now on practice and precision work are all that are needed to produce a well balanced, obedient and useful driving horse. As his responses improve and he becomes adept at his trot, more work should be done on his transitions and ability to move on immediately when required. With improved balance and head carriage, work at the extended trot can be carried out, always making certain that it is not overdone. A sure way to achieve a sprawling, uncoordinated and unsightly gait is to ask for too much speed too soon. Impulsion must come from the hind quarters, and without good impulsion the front action will not be satisfactory or pleasing. The horse must work off his hocks and as his training progresses, he should be pushed on from the rear and restrained slightly in front to produce the type of action typical of his breed and expected of him.

The walk must be practiced as well, to develop a gait that is elastic and rapid—a slow, dull, lifeless walk is not going to cover any ground or look anything but uninteresting. A good walk is a basis for all other gaits and requires much practice and work to achieve. It is easier to train a horse to walk properly after he has learned to trot satisfactorily.

Halts should be practiced regularly and the colt taught to stand quietly in the line up position. He should not fuss, fidget or move around, and this is taught gradually from the very beginning on the lines. The time span in which he will stand still increases steadily with practice until he can be expected to stand for the amount of time necessary in the show ring. Depending upon his breed and the stance required he should be taught at the same time to stand squarely or in a stretched position and to maintain that stance.

After a month or so in the cart, the colt is ready to be taught to back up. This is done first on the ground, backing him up by his halter and saying the words, "back up." Always use the same words when asking a horse to do a maneuver because it helps him understand what is required. Next, with open bridle and standing behind the colt on long lines, pull gently back and tell him, "back up." As soon as he takes even one step, release and praise him. The back up should be taught using the pull and release system—the colt backs one step with each pull and halts with the release. In this manner, the number of steps can be controlled exactly and the horse is never in danger of running away backwards. When the colt will back up readily in the open bridle, the driving bridle should be substituted and the process repeated. Then he can be hitched to the cart and asked to back it up. At first the trainer should stay on the ground allow the colt to back the empty cart, as this is new to him and a bit difficult at the start. When he can back the empty cart easily, then the driver can get in and expect the colt to be able to back up without a problem. Care must be taken not to ask for too much backing up at any one time, as it is a maneuver disliked by a horse and not one he uses in his natural environment. Two or three "backs" in any training session should be enough.

Work in a four-wheeled buggy may be done at any time now, as the colt has become proficient in the cart at the gaits required of him. To the colt there will be very little difference except that there is no weight on the shafts in a four-wheeled buggy. But to the driver, if unfamiliar with such a vehicle, the difference will be considerable since he can no longer turn anywhere at any time. He must plan ahead and allow room to turn and be careful not to jackknife the wheels in doing so. With a well-trained and steady horse there is no difficulty learning to handle a four-wheeled buggy, and the drivers' reactions and reflexes soon become attuned to its limitations and requirements. Backing up can present a problem though, as extreme steadiness and control are necessary to back straight. Practice makes perfect in this case.

Now we are prepared to go on to some advanced training and achieve the necessary gaits and qualifications required for each class and each breed of horse and pony. With such a good basic conditioning and elementary training under his belt the colt will have no problem following through into higher education.

In the following chapters, each breed will be discussed thoroughly as well as the type of harness, vehicles, and qualifications necessary. The required performance expected and demanded by the show ring will be dealt with and training methods and techniques will be described in detail.

Advanced Training for the Show Ring

Now that your horse is driving well in harness, you can begin to concentrate his training along the proper lines to achieve the requirements necessitated by his breed. Up to this point all breeds are started the same way, but once their elementary schooling is satisfactory they must be encouraged to display the distinctive qualifications of their heritage. Each breed of horse has a "way of going" that is special to that breed and which distinguishes it from all other breeds. In some cases these differences may be very slight, but they exist and the true exponent will be quick to point them out.

As mentioned in the previous book, all show horses wear equipment designated by their Breed Associations and in conjunction with CHSA or AHSA rules. It should be pointed out that this ruling is *strictly* for show purposes. Any breed can be driven in any well fitted harness for other purposes *outside* of the show ring.

In the following chapters we will attempt to lay down some guide lines for the beginner to enable him to proceed with more advanced training in a manner designed to turn out a show horse. As each horse is an individual, it must be borne in mind that these are just "guide lines" and should be interpreted with your own animal's temperament and conditioning in mind. What one horse will accept quietly and readily may excite and frighten another horse to a degree verging on hysteria. A good trainer instinctively senses the reaction his horse may exhibit and should be able to predict fairly accurately his response to a given situation. He will also know his horse well enough to deal with the situation in a manner designed to calm and reassure the animal. This may take the form of a gentle pat and soothing voice or a sharp command and a slap, depending entirely upon the makeup of the horse and the problem encountered. Therefore, as you read the following pages you should be translating in your own mind the information as it pertains to your horse.

2
THE ARABIAN HORSE

Arabian horses are noted for their intelligence, courage, endurance, and affectionate nature. Their classic dished face and high tail carriage are distinctive identification for even the uninitiated. Possessing a trot that can vary from a free, easy ground covering action to a brilliant, animated and floating gait, the Arabian makes a very pleasant and desirable harness horse. His trotting gait is characterized by a free shoulder action, forefeet shooting forwards with a full floating movement and powerful hock action. His hind legs must be brought well under him so that he is indeed "working well off his hocks."

Arabians are shown in harness in three categories: formal driving, pleasure driving, and roadster. Each category has its specific requirements as to harness, vehicle, type and way of going. The training therefore must also vary with the class. In all classes the Arabian is shown with a full mane and tail—he is not braided. His bridle path is usually shaved back about six inches.

Formal Driving

The formal driving horse must be an upstanding individual with neck set high on a good sloping shoulder. Good length of neck is desirable in this class and withers should be at least as high as croup; if higher all the better. The greater length of forearm and shoulder contributes greatly to the free movement necessary in this event. He should have a good top line because in harness it is all in plain sight and not covered up as is the case under saddle. He should be a high-couraged animal, lively, animated and able to show brilliance at all gaits. It stands to reason that to have the foregoing characteristics the horse must be a real athlete. If the horse is excessively quiet and relaxed he will not fare well in a formal driving class.

The gaits called for in this event are the "walk," and "animated natural trot". The class is judged on presence, manners, quality and conformation; qualifications listed in order of their importance. Class specifications are always listed in the order of their importance as well as judged in that order.

The walk in a formal driving class should be true, rapid and elastic. There must be no tendency to jog, slow or drag. The horse should walk briskly with collection and his joints should flex vigorously in a springy manner.

The animated natural trot is an extremely brilliant trot. The forefeet shoot forward and dwell an instant at full stretch with floating movement before touching the ground (not round action). This is combined with hock action that is powerful and well-raised, while the hind leg is brought forward with a swinging stride. This gait demands a high degree of collection and necessitates the greatest output of energy at both ends of the horse.

The other requirements of this class are to stand quietly and back readily. Arabians are not always allowed grooms at their heads in a line up and are required to stand quietly without fidgeting or fussing. When asked to back, they should do so willingly and freely and with controlled cadence.

Equipment

Now that we know and understand the requirements and regulations concerning the formal driving class of Arabians, let us look at the harness and equipment necessary for this very showy event. The obvious elegance and quality of the horse who attains formal driving status must be matched by his harness, buggy and appointments.

The rule book states that Arabian Formal Driving Horses are to be "shown in light harness, bridle with blinkers and overcheck, snaffle bit (straight or jointed) to a four-wheeled show vehicle."

The standard "light show harness" includes a running martingale. The blinkers, backpad and browband (and sometimes the chest section of the breast collar) are made of quality patent leather. The entire harness is black with the exception of the hand parts of the reins which should be tan. It is equally correct to use all russet reins. The backpad is fine and narrower than everyday pleasure harness, no wider than 2½" made of top quality leather and finely sewn. The bellyband should buckle on each side, have leather buckle guards, be of the folded and sewn type, and have fine well-shaped wrap straps of no more than ¾ inch width. The crupper strap should be in proportional width and the crupper must be well stuffed, comfortable and soft. The breast collar is of the folded and sewn style with overstitched top layer and traces are sometimes made round back to the trace ends, which must be flat. The reins back to the tan handparts may be of rounded leather as are the forked ends of the running martingale. The bridle is made very fine and of narrower leather than its corresponding pleasure or training counterpart. The overdraw checkrein is usually connected to its own small check bit and both bits are of good quality nickel or stainless steel. The cheeks of the show bridle should be box loop style while blinker stays should be round and well-shaped and the blinkers well cupped. The harness should have solid brass hardware throughout.

The four-wheeled show buggy is usually of side-bar style with 26-inch heavy duty chromed show wheels and chromed seat railing, reach and springs. The box is narrow, seating just one person and its glossy finish reflects the many coats of paint that have gone into it (sometimes up to 21 thin coats!). The dash is of patent leather and the seat cushion has a small leather apron. The floor carpeting and the seat cushion are normally of a deep maroon or wine shade. The shafts are of second growth hickory and should be well ironed with leather sleeves from the tips back about two feet. The fancier singletrees have brass trace hooks at each end and the stops on the outside of the shafts may be of brass also.

The overall effect achieved by both harness and buggy is one of extreme elegance. This arrangement is beautifully suited to exposing all the natural beauty of the Arabian horse performing his exquisitely lovely "animated natural trot."

Training

Now we have the requirements for type of horse, gaits called for, harness and buggy needed. All that remains is to bring the horses' training up to the performance standard necessary. If the trainer has followed the previous chapter's work assiduously he should have no difficulty achieving this level of performance.

We have our young colt, our formal driving prospect, driving well in our cart (or show buggy) moving freely and willingly and showing fairly quick response to our commands. Up to this point we have allowed him to trot along at a calm, easy speed concentrating on obtaining balance, cadence and lightness. Now we must begin to collect him and ask for some animation. We want our colt to work well off his hocks, in other words with his hind legs reaching well under him, and to be light and airy in front. At this time we will shorten his checkrein a hole or two to begin to shift the weight off his front end. As he trots along on light contact take more "feel" or contact with your reins while clucking him on and encouraging him with your voice to some excitement. With this added impulsion from the hind end and the restraining (but gentle) contact from the bit, he has only one way to go and that is up. This brilliant float is what we are striving to achieve, but we must not ask our colt to continue with such vigor for more than a round of the ring at this early stage. His muscles and timing must be built up gradually to a point where he is able to cope with the demands of this "animated natural trot."

Much work is required at the transitions from ordinary trot to this animated trot. The colt has to learn to respond instantly and switch to this gait upon command. You will have to vary the length of his checkrein until you find the best length for ultimate performance, but be careful not to have it too short or you may frustrate him to the point of ruin. He cannot perform properly with too tight a checkrein. As the animated trot can only be achieved when the horse is at his point of greatest output of energy, you must take care not to overdo any workout. Continue to encourage him to push on with animation and check his speed with half halts and squeezes on the reins. Remember that a horse will always look brilliant as long as he is putting more impulsion in the rear than he is using up in forward motion in front. Never keep a steady pull on your horse's mouth, this will just make it hard. Try to use small tugs or squeezes; sometimes one rein at a time to avoid hurting the horse's mouth. As a rule, Arabians have very light, sensitive mouths and respond well to gentleness.

The walk must also be a vigorous gait. It should be brisk, collected, and springy. We achieve this in the same manner as the animated trot. We ask for impulsion from the hind end and take back with the reins so that the overall effect is the "true, rapid, and elastic" gait described in the Rule Book. A discreet play of the reins is necessary to keep our horse to this collected gait and no faster and will require considerable practice.

The reverse, back up and line up, are done in the manner already described in great detail in previous chapters.

Head Set and Work in a Bitting Rig

At this point in his training the colt should spend considerable time in a bitting rig to develop a good head set and a soft quick response to the bit. We will use the bitting rig in a slightly different manner than that described in the earlier work and will vary the use of the side reins and side checks to achieve improved flexion and elevation. Put the bitting harness on the colt leaving both side reins and side checks undone. This is best done in his stall as that is where he is going to wear it. Now using the solid side checkrein (without the elastic insert), run it through the ring on the center front of the backpad and snap on each side of his bit. Adjust this rein until the colt has to arch his neck and tuck his chin in somewhat to keep the rein slack. Be careful not to make it too tight—it is a training, not a torture device! This teaches the colt to give until the rein is slack—his reward. If he resists and pulls he punishes himself by hurting his mouth. He soon learns to give and stand flexed. Leave him to walk around his stall with the bitting harness on in this fashion for 15 to 20 minutes, then take him out and work him. Two or three sessions a week in this equipment will see a big improvement in his head set. The muscle on the top of his neck will stretch and lengthen gradually while the muscle underneath will loosen up and become less muscular, resulting in a clean, well shaped throat latch.

Sometimes a horse will insist on resisting the set described above by trying to poke his nose out. If he does, snap on your side reins and adjust them to prevent this.

When your colt is up in the bitting rig, don't go too far away for a long period. You must keep an eye on him from time to time as he can get himself into all sorts of mischief. Some horses will get up against the side of the stall and rub the harness off to one side, thus pulling the side reins crooked. We don't want him to stand for any time in this manner as straightness is a must in the show ring and horses learn all to easily to become crooked to one side or another.

While on the subject of a good head set it should be mentioned that unless the horse has a lean, clean throat latch he cannot flex properly. A horse that has built up a big layer of fat on the jowl and throat is physically unable to flex his head and neck. A fat jowl also looks very unsightly and often spoils the look of an otherwise beautiful animal. This fat must be sweat off in some manner. There are many jowl sweats and hoods available today and some work for some animals while others find a different type more useful. I like the rubber full neck sweat or partial length for my own animals. I work them in the neck sweat and have had excellent results. One must take care to wash both horse and rubber neck sweat after each use or the horse could become scalded and sore.

A jowl sweat tends in some cases to just push the fat to each side rather than sweat it off and has the annoying habit of rubbing out the mane on top into the bargain. They sometimes aggravate the horse, who starts rubbing

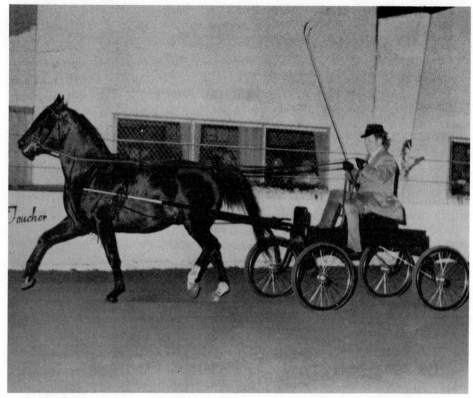

Formal Driving Arabian horse. "Alfajr" #51328, purebred Arabian stallion owned by J. E. "Red" Fadling, Flying R Ranch, Olympia, Washington.

head up and down—a habit that can continue on into his work in harness. The jowl hood that goes right over his head and ears is more comfortable for the horse but the results are rather "so-so"—I have never actually felt the horse sweating in either of these jowl sweats. Some experimenting is obviously necessary until you find the most suitable and useful type for your animal.

Pleasure Driving

The pleasure driving ·prospect must meet only one absolutely vital requirement and that is one of temperament. He should have other attributes such as type and style but temperament is paramount. He must not appear lazy nor high strung and should convey the appearance of enjoying his work. Good conformation is an asset since it automatically makes his job easier for him. He must have good Arab type, of course, but the extreme perfection desired in Formal Driving is not necessary in this class.

The gaits called for in the Pleasure Driving class are flat-footed walk, slow trot and a fast trot. The class is judged on manners, quality and performance in that order of importance.

The walk must be flat-footed, brisk, and true. It should look like the horse is actually going somewhere and be a ground covering gait. It must be true, i.e., have a definite one-two-three-four beat and must never degenerate into an amble or joggy motion. He must not look like a "dead head" at the walk, yet he should not be pulling on the reins.

The slow trot is a well-cadenced, easy, free moving gait, not collected or as slow as the western jog, yet not quite as fast as the trot under english saddle. It should look effortless yet be ground covering and give the impression that the horse could keep on going all day. It should be driven with light but positive contact—no flapping or sagging reins!

The fast trot is a bit of a misnomer because speed is not only undesirable, but extreme speed is penalized. A fast trot is brisk, smart, well-cadenced, balanced and showy. Although the extreme vigor of the Formal Driving Horse is not desired, the horse still must work off his hocks and the impulsion produced will be reflected in the forelegs floating forward elegantly yet effortlessly. His stride should never be short or choppy but rather long and free.

In pleasure driving, the overall smoothness and consistency of performance is of most importance. The impression should be that anyone could enjoy driving the animal with easy control and a minimum of effort.

Pleasure driving horses are also required to stand quietly in the line up and to back readily.

Equipment

The harness used for this class is similar to that used in Formal Driving, but need not be so fine. The pleasure horse, even though shown in a light cart or buggy, is expected to pull heavier loads while out driving in the countryside. Actually, while in the show ring he will be dressed up more than usual, so he can easily be shown—and correctly so—in the formal driving harness. However, it is not an absolute necessity and more preferable (and economical) is a slightly less fancy show harness. The bridle will be the same, but the choice of using the extra check bit is optional. As extreme action is not called for, the head carriage need not be so high, therefore the overcheck may be attached to the driving bit and be at a comfortable length for smooth and easy performance.

The breast collar is more useful if it has flat traces and they may be either buckled or sewn on to the collar. The traces and collar ought to be of fairly narrow width to be showy but can be thicker to obtain extra strength. The backpad should be the same width and trimmed with patent leather, and the bellyband need not be the fancy folded and sewn style, but can be flat with loops to guide the wrap straps. Crupper and crupper strap will be the same, and the reins can be flat black leather back to the tan hand parts rather than the rounded style. The martingale will look a bit prettier with rounded forks but if cut and edged skillfully by a proper harness maker, flat narrow forks look just as showy. Again solid brass hardware should be used throughout.

Pleasure driving horses may be shown to either a two or four-wheeled vehicle. The Rule Book states ". . . shall be shown to a suitable two or four-wheeled vehicle, the type of which is optional to the Show Committee, but which type must be specified in the prize list." If a two-wheeled cart is specified you may use any two-wheeler, but keep in mind that it is a show and use a cart that is in proportion to and enhances the look of your horse. If a four-wheeled vehicle is called for, the usual style is the fine harness show buggy as used in the Formal Driving Class. Old fashioned buggies certainly have audience appeal and are ideally suited to costume classes, but to be the only one in this type of buggy while everyone else is in a show buggy is to stand out like a sore thumb. The exception to this would be a "pleasure driving class—ladies to drive"—in which case the old fashioned buggy with the lady driver suitably attired in a matching vintage costume would definitely be an eye appealing entry.

Training

To bring our young colt's performance level up to this pleasure driving standard is a very easy task indeed since it follows the work done and level achieved in previous chapters.

Our young colt is driving fluidly, quietly and responsively and has become well balanced and flexed with the figures and circles done both at slow gaits and at a faster pace. All that remains to achieve pleasure driving standards is to perfect his transitions and to give him some dress rehearsals in a show ring with other horses in carts—perferably when no show is going on. He needs to attain a carefree attitude so that he may perform cheerfully and with complete understanding of what his task in the show ring is to entail and this he can only get from experience.

Pleasure Driving Arabian Horse. "Kae Galliano+," #067800, Purebred Arabian gelding owned and driven by John Follgard, Calgary, Alberta. Winner at Saskatchewan, Alberta, British Columbia and Montana in pleasure driving classes.

Our colt has already learned to back up properly with the pull and release method and he should also be adept at standing in line with so much practice during his training days.

Roadster

The Roadster class is a relatively new one to the Arabian breed and one that gives much scope to the stride and build of the animal. In this class the "Drinker of the Wind" is allowed to move out freely and to display the speed and coordinated form of which he is so capable. Our roadster prospect should display a free and easy stride, brilliance, presence and a keenness or desire to move on. He must not be lazy, dull-eyed or of a sedentary nature—these qualifications will not be of any use in a roadster class. He should have a good sloping shoulder, deep chest, and strong, well proportioned hind quarters. His ability to perform well in the roadster division will stem from these characteristics.

The classes for roadsters are open, maiden, novice, limit, stallions, mares, and geldings. The gaits called for in each of these classes are jog trot, road gait, and then at speed. The classes are judged on performance, speed, quality, and manners in that order of consideration. In junior, ladies, or amateur classes the order of consideration is manners, performance, speed, and quality.

The roadster is shown to a two wheeled bike or sulky, sometimes called a roadster cart.

The jog trot is a medium speed gait, ground covering, but not fast. Horses enter the ring clockwise at the jog trot in each class and should stay on the rail at this speed without passing. At this speed it is almost always possible to space yourself out to maintain a position on the rail. With the rest of the class entering the ring steadily it becomes most awkward and often dangerous if those already in the ring start passing and driving on faster than that called for. Once everyone is in the ring and the gate shut, the driver should pick a spot on the rail and try to maintain his distance from the horse in front.

The jog trot should display some brilliance and a real freedom of movement. The horse should be slightly collected, have his head fairly well set, and should be up on the bit but not pulling or showing signs of being difficult to control. The road gait is much faster and here the horse must show his speed without losing form or cadence. He must go well into his turns without side-reining or breaking gait. Any scrambling or tendency to pace on the corners is a serious fault. He should bend in his corners looking inward, not turning his head to the outside (a fault seen in most classes and especially when shown at speed.) He must work well off his hind quarters and show strong true impulsion. His front end should be light and airy and his head high and well set. His ears should be forward and alert, never sour and pinned back. At this gait he must show control and not pull too hard or appear difficult to keep down to the road gait. Horses tend to anticipate the "drive on" command and sometimes become impatient and excited and very difficult to hold back. When asked to "drive on" the horse should make the transition smoothly and without breaking cadence. While travelling at top speed he must go in form and the turns are even more important at this gait. He must corner flat and come out fast and true, not become sprawly-gaited, strung out, or break into a canter for a few strides. He must look into the direction of the turn and not to the outside and his quarters must follow truly in line rather than falling in on the turns. The roadster must stand in the line up quietly and back readily if request. Headers are not allowed in a roadster class and the horse must display good line up manners and sensibility. He should stand square and not fidget or fuss, or throw his head trying to loosen the checkrein. He must remain checked up in the line up.

Equipment

The harness worn in the roadster class should be a light, fine type, but strong and able to stand up to the stress put on it during the speedy transitions and corners. The bridle usually has box loop cheeks, square blinkers, overdraw checkrein, noseband or caveson and a snaffle bit. The check bit can be either jointed or straight. The breast collar is very fine, about 1¼ inches and has sewn on traces for added strength and safety. A margingale is worn on all roadsters and should be quite fine, with the forks either rounded or beaded. The backpad should be fairly narrow, no wider than 2½ inches and have open shaft loops, wrap straps on the belly band and thimbles attached to the dees of the backpad. The crupper strap is fine and the crupper is sewn on. Reins can be either all russett or black back to the tan handparts. The buckle end of the reins should have steel reinforcement. Breeching is not worn in roadster to bike classes. It is customary to have considerable patent leather on a roadster harness which adds to the elegance of the turnout. The hardware should be brass.

Quarter boots are usually worn in roadster classes. These are hinged boots and are worn on the front feet. Bell boots may be worn since they will afford protection from an overreach, but the hinged quarter boots will promote a better action. They must, however, be unweighted. An Arabian is not permitted to have leaded or weighted quarter boots. Make sure the boots fit the horse! If they are too small they will pinch him and eventually make him sore and short-striding. If they are too large they will flop halfway up his leg and be so awkward that they will discourage him from moving out properly.

The bike called for in these classes is a small, light, two-wheeled cart or sulky. The wheels run in forks for added strength and the driver sits in a small seat over the axle with his feet up in stirrups on either side. The horse's hind feet pass underneath his seat when trotting at speed and the driver's hands are only inches away from the horse's flanks at times because the horse is hitched quite close in a road bike. This of course leads to a very quick and positive control.

The driver in a roadster class wears silks or "colors." This consists of a jacket and cap of matching colors; usually the colors of the stable owner. The slacks worn are usually of ordinary everyday color and style and the driver will find riding boots to be comfortable and safe while driving with his feet up in the stirrups.

Training

Our roadster prospect has already mastered the basic gaits as described in the earlier chapters and has shown the potential and qualifications looked for in a roadster. Now we must perfect his gaits and teach him to trot at ever increasing speed in proper form.

First we must look carefully at his feet and way of going. He must move absolutely straight and not wing or paddle or else he is bound to come to grief at fast speeds. He will be almost certain to hit himself in the corners and will be unable to display a clean, true gait if his front feet are dishing in or out or describing an arc with each step. Have him trimmed or shod to go straight and keep a record of the length of toe and heel, the angle of the foot, and the weight of his shoes so you can reproduce the effect you find best or change it to something that works better. Angle and weight are very critical where great speed is required. A light shoe will be best suited for this class, as the Arabian is not expected to produce high action such as the Hackney or American Saddlebred.

Introduce the horse to boots. He should wear boots during his training both for protection and to promote a higher, cleaner type of action. Either bell boots or quarter boots may be used; the latter will give slightly better results for this class. Jog him in boots, not asking for any faster gait until he becomes accustomed to the feel of the boots and learns to handle himself in them. A good jog trot is very essential for a roadster and as you jog, start setting him up a bit and asking for some animation and collection.

Be very observant in the turns. Be sure he shows no inclination to side-rein or turn his head outwards and his quarters to the inside. If he does exhibit this very undesirable trait, drive him in small circles for a minute or two, forcing his head to the inside. He must learn to balance properly in his corners and if he cannot do it at a jog trot there is no point in trying it at a faster gait. It is absolutely essential that he corner flat and true.

Now we ask for a bit more speed on the straight stretches and take back on the corners. It is easier to instigate and control animation on the straights. Remember—the faster he goes the more support he needs from your hands. His checkrein should be fairly high and tight by now and he should go with a high and well set head, chin tucked nicely but not pulling hard. Work in a bitting rig will be of great benefit in achieving a good head set and in teaching him to give to the pull. Put the bitting rig on without using the drops on the bridle for the side checks as we have been doing up until now. Run the solid checkrein from one side of his bit through the ring on the backpad and onto the other side of his bit. Adjust tight enough to achieve almost the height and set you require, leaving it so that if he gives (tucks) there is no pressure on him and his head will be where you want it. Leave him in his stall wearing this rig for twenty to thirty minutes, then take him straight out and drive him. Twice a week in the bitting rig should be most useful in achieving a good head set.

Keep sending the horse on and taking him back softly, never with jerks, using your voice and clucks to excite him to an effort of brilliance and animation. By now he should be doing a pretty good road gait and learning balance in his turns. Make sure you send him right into his corners; don't allow him to start cutting his corners or trying to turn before the actual corner.

Much practice is necessary at the transition between the jog trot and road gait. Jog around a few times, then send him up into a road gait—his transition must become smooth, elastic and instantaneous. Practice the transition back to a jog trot and once again up to road gait. This is where your fine control is accomplished, and in the show ring at any speed including "drive on" you must create the impression of being able at any time to come back to a jog trot with ease. Good manners without severe bitting and absolute control without undue force and pulling are requisite.

Once you have your horse doing a well-balanced and speedy road gait with fast flat corners, you can begin to ask for full speed on the straights for short bursts. Again, the transitions are most important and will need much practice. At full speed the horse will require great support from the driver's hands and very subtle yet firm assistance in the corners. You will have to experiment to find out just how fast you can go into your corners and still come out flat and true. At the first sign of a break or scrambling action take him back to a speed he can control and settle him before attempting another corner. His speed must always be in form and he has to work off his hocks. Any tendency to string out behind or dragging and trailing the hind quarters through the corners is a serious fault and one that will make a balanced gait impossible.

The making of a roadster—a good one—takes time and many a top roadster prospect is ruined by too much hurry. The horse has to work up to top speed very gradually, learning to balance and keep form with every increment in speed. If you can work out on a half-mile track or on a country road for awhile where there are few sharp, short corners it will be most advantageous for your horse. Here he can learn to trot at great speed without having to worry about keeping his balance in corners. It is also very good for his mental attitude to get out and really stretch in a free fast trot with new scenery. Horses do become ring sour, especially when required to go at speed in a small enclosure.

In the show ring the roadster is only required to drive at top speed in one direction of the ring—counter clockwise—but it is a good plan to train both ways at home to keep your horse straight. It will help his balance and make it easier for him in the long run.

In the lineup the roadster will have to stand quietly, unheaded and checked up. Some practice should be done at home along these lines. He will also be subjected to a clapping, screaming, noisy crowd. Any way you can simulate these conditions in your home ring will be a great help in preparing the horse for this condition in the show ring.

The presence of one or more horses in your home ring will be of great help as well. It is very exciting for your horse when trotting at full speed to have another horse pass him. It may cause him to break or get out of control. You should try to accustom him to these and other show ring situations during his training at home. Once he has been subjected to a given situation a few times it is no longer as frightening or exciting to him and will be less likely to cause a problem in the actual show ring.

Your roadster should now be ready for his first show and all that is needed is a few shows under his belt to perfect his technique *and* yours!

3
THE MORGAN HORSE

The Morgan horse, often called "The Pride and Product of America", is perhaps the most versatile of all breeds. Equally at home and at ease under english or western saddle, in pleasure or work harness, he combines ability with disposition. Probably the most distinguishing characteristic of the Morgan is his body conformation. From shoulder to buttock is considerably longer than his height, due to his extremely long sloping shoulder and well developed croup. A very compact and muscular horse, he usually possesses a lovely, fine clean cut head set on a well crested neck. Displaying a trot that can vary from an easy going, free, elastic stride to an animated brilliant and high stepping action he is an ideal harness horse. His recognized stamina, docility, and willingness combine with vigor, alertness, and spirit to produce an effect of great reliability—hence his tremendous popularity as an all around family pet.

Morgans are shown in harness in four different events: Park horse in harness, Pleasure driving, Roadster to Bike and the fourth requirement of the Justin Morgan class—to pull a stone boat with 500 pounds minimum weight a distance of six feet in work harness. In addition to these recognized classes, many shows also feature a Gay 90s class for Morgans in which a good percentage of entries are shown in harness.

Morgans are always shown with full mane and tail.

Park Horse in Harness

The Park Horse in harness should be a high-headed, bold, and airy moving animal. He should move with brilliance, animation, and collection and exhibit good action without a forced appearance. He should look through his bridle with presence and eagerness and exhibit a balanced, powerful stride while at the same time exuding an impression of gentleness and controlled high spirits.

The gaits called for in this event are the animated trot and the animated walk. The class is judged on performance, presence, quality, manners and suitability as a stylish harness horse, type and conformation.

The animated trot should be a square collected balanced gait of a definite two-beat cadence. The flight of the front foot should approach the arc of a circle and the stride should be of a height and length that can be performed with rapidity, elasticity and precision and with considerable shoulder movement. The hock action should be powerful and well under the horse to balance the front end. The stride of the park harness horse is usually longer than that of the park saddle horse. It is a stronger going stride, bold but not fast. Excessive speed is undesirable and will be penalized. The horse should execute the animated trot in a gentle and free manner neither pulling on the reins nor keeping them slack. He should be driven with light positive contact.

The animated walk should be rapid, collected, animated, elastic, true and in a straight line. There must be no tendency to jig or amble and the horse must not appear sluggish or strung out. He should exhibit an eager expression, ears pricked, neck flexed, and the impression that he is actually going somewhere.

In the line up Park Harness Morgans are allowed a header, i.e., an attendant to stand at their heads. This attendant must not have a whip and is allowed to stand the entry on its feet and thereafter remain at least two paces distant from the head when the judge is inspecting the horse.

Equipment

The harness worn by the Park Harness horse should match the elegance of the animal. Although it is not required to be quite as fine as that described earlier for the Formal Driving Arabian horse, it would be correct to wear such a harness. The Morgan horse is extremely fortunate in the lenient attitude towards specific harness shown by the association concerned. Although Park Harness horses are usually seen to be wearing a snaffle bit and overdraw checkrein style, Morgans are allowed a choice of several styles of bridle. They can be shown in snaffle bit with overdraw checkrein or snaffle, liverpool or buxton bit with side checks. If using a snaffle bit with overdraw checkrein it is customary to also wear a running martingale. With this style, square blinkers are usually best suited to the overall appearance. This wide range of choice gives the Morgan owner or trainer a chance to use the type best suited to his horse's conformation and way of going. With their distinctive and high crested necks many Morgans look and show best in side checks. When side checks are employed round blinkers should be worn, and a liverpool bit is more complimentary than a snaffle. A small check bit should be used in conjunction with the main bit no matter which type of bridle is worn. This bit may be either straight or jointed.

The harness should be of fine stylish quality, and the decision regarding round or flat traces, round or flat reins, or the amount of patent leather is left up to the owner. Round reins and traces are fancier but much more difficult to obtain than the other types nowadays.

With his somewhat more muscular build and conformation, the Morgan can wear a harness less narrow in all its components than the Arabian and have it look just as fine. Brass hardware throughout is, again, a must for a show harness.

The Park Harness Morgan should be hitched to a light four-wheeled show buggy. The design may be of side bar style or regular leaf spring type. It should be an elegant buggy with considerable chrome trim and deep rich paint job along the same lines as the fine harness buggy described for the Arabian Formal Driving class.

Training

The training of the Park Harness Morgan continues the training program already begun in the previous chapters. Our colt has already demonstrated his park harness tendencies in style, action and presence; now we must "hone" his performance ability to the utmost.

We begin by shortening his checkrein a hole or two and asking for short bursts of extreme impulsion at the trot. We cluck him on, sending him up into his bridle while at the same time restraining him gently. The result is a balanced, high-actioned, animated trot with front legs folding in elegant rhythm and hind legs reaching well underneath with a powerful hock action. This animated trot comes very easily to a Morgan and requires very little urging. His natural good action can be enhanced and improved by shoeing and by the use of "rattlers" or similar aids. Rattlers are of various types, the most common being small, round, wooden balls made of vita lignum threaded on a leather bracelet which buckles around the horse's pastern below the fetlock joint. Chain rattlers are also a humane type and consist of small, light weight chain making a circle around the pastern, with the ends buckled together by a small leather strap. These rattlers move up and down jiggling around as the horse trots and the movement encourages higher action. The higher action obtained develops muscles and habit with the long term result of a higher and snappier action. Rattlers are strictly a training device and may not be worn or used in the show ring.

Shoeing can be of great value in producting higher and better action. The length of foot and the weight and shape of the shoe can play a large part in the way the horse moves and steps. Up to a point, heavier shoes and a longer foot will produce higher action but after that point this extra weight becomes a cumbersome burden. The horse's action becomes clumsy, laboring and pounding, and often is accompanied by winging or paddling. A judge will severely fault a horse that is overshod in this manner. In Park Harness classes there is no specific shoe weight limit but the length of toe must not exceed five inches including pad and shoe.

The combination of proper shoeing, training aids such as rattlers, and driving technique will produce the animated trot (and walk) required for the Park Harness class. The method described earlier to produce short bursts of vigorous impulsion will be extended to longer and longer periods until the horse is capable of displaying this animation with good form and cadence for several rounds of the ring. We must be careful to achieve this end without loss of hock action or any tendency to string out behind. His weight must never shift to his forehand or he will become heavy in the front end and lose all airiness of action and movement. The driver has to always be on the look out for loss of impulsion that will result in a shift of balance of weight and correct the situation before that happens.

The animated walk is achieved in the same manner as the trot. It should be collected, elastic, and rapid, and the driver's hands must be very sensitive and his reflexes fast to achieve optimum performance. If he pushes on too hard the horse will break into a trot and if he pulls too hard the horse will slow down and lose all animation. Thus the happy medium is a feel of the reins that varies from moment to moment and becomes an instictive technique gained from experience. One of the requirements for the animated walk is that the horse must move in a straight line. It is surprising how many horses fail in this qualification. If his training has progressed along the lines discussed in this book there will be little likelihood of a problem in this area, but the drive must make certain that his horse meets the requirement.

If the horse is two-tracking or oscillating down the straights, go back to some basic training with figures and circles until balance and form are established with the horse going up into his bridle. Work in a bitting rig will be of great benefit in this area and will assist in straightening the horse.

Some faults to watch out for at the animated walk are sour ears, fighting

Park Harness Morgan horse. "Hillcrest Leader" owned by Art Perry Jr., Intrepid Farms, Carpinteria, Calif., driven by James Wigle. This sixteen-year-old stallion continues to show and win with the style and animation required for this class.

the bit, tossing the head, and tongue lolling. Any one of these attitudes will indicate that the horse is not going kindly or willingly.

Pleasure Driving

The Pleasure Driving Morgan should have the same excellence of type and presence as the Park Harness horse. He will have less animation and must display an absolutely agreeable attitude at all gaits. It has been said that the difference between a Park Harness horse and a Pleasure Driving horse is not so much what he does but the manner in which he does it.

The head of the pleasure driving horse is not carried quite as high and the flexion is not as great as in Park Harness, but the Morgan pleasure horse does *not* travel with his neck low and his nose poked out.

The gaits called for in pleasure driving are a walk, slow trot and extended trot. The class is judged on performance, manners, quality, type and conformation. Horses may be asked to back; this requirement left to the judge's discretion. One attendant without a whip is allowed in the ring to head each horse.

The walk in a pleasure driving class should be flat-footed, rapid, elastic and showy. Since it is the gait actually used most in pleasure work, it is important in the scoring of a pleasure class. A horse that won't settle down and walk, or one with a slow, sluggish spiritless walk is not likely to be a winner. The desired gait is characterized by alert interest, expressive ears and complete willingness. The horse *must* do a flat-footed walk; a four beat gait free of any jogging or tendency to pace. (Any tendency to pace is a serious fault.) At the walk, the Morgan should show a distinctive flexing of his pasterns, move forward in a straight line and look where he is going. The pleasure driving walk is more relaxed than that of the Park Harness.

The slow trot is a graceful, square, balanced gait. The horse should move freely and easily with a two-beat cadence. He should land lightly and give the impression that he could travel a long distance without tiring. The slow trot must never be strung out or lifeless but must maintain sufficient collection to keep both form and style. An attitude of cheerfulness, willingness, and a natural athletic ability should be apparent in a pleasure trot.

The extended trot is a faster, more extended gait with free forward impulsion. The horse will be working more off his hocks and a powerful forward and upward thrust should be transmitted to the front legs. The extended trot is a real ground covering gait but action and form must not be sacrificed for speed. Considerable emphasis is given to the horse's ability to move freely, therefore the length of the checkrein will be of importance. Because of his type he will have a relatively high head carriage, but care must be taken that the checkrein does not interfere with a relaxed and free way of going.

If the judge requests the entires to back up, the maneuver should be done willingly, straight, and with controlled rhythm. Rushing, throwing the head, crookedness and refusal to back are considered serious faults.

Equipment

The harness worn by the pleasure driving Morgan in the show ring is usually the same as that worn by the Park Harness Morgan. It may be of slightly heavier leather but should be of stylish show caliber. Again, the type of bit and checkrein is optional and should be suited to the horse. The use of rounded leather parts such as traces or reins is not considered necessary in this class, and in some cases the flat leather will be more in keeping with the vehicle.

In pleasure driving classes, horses may be shown to an appropriate vehicle of *either* two or four wheels. If a four-wheeled show buggy is to be used it should be the same as that previously described for the Park Harness horse. If a two-wheeler is your choice it should be in proportion to the horse and in keeping with the harness used. A flimsy, small, and obviously fragile cart is not suitable to be pulled by a strong, muscular and powerful Morgan beauty. There are many carts on the market that will afford the driver the choice of one suitable for the job at hand. The show ring cart is usually fancier, has more chrome and seats only one or two persons, while the pleasure cart used at home is much sturdier, less fancy and more useful. Cross-country carts are very popular for home use. Whatever the choice, the cart used in the show ring should be clean with its chrome gleaming and correctly turned out.

The overall effect of the turnout should be one of pleasure, grace and beauty.

Training

The pleasure driving trot requires very little further training than our young colt now possesses. We will collect him a bit more and perhaps shorten his checkrein a hole or two, but for this event his training is already fairly adequate. He should be doing the slow trot at the performance standard required and his extended trot should need merely to be collected a bit and his cadence steadied.

The action of the pleasure horse is not usually as high as his Park counterpart, but nevertheless pleasing action is required. The use of rattlers and a good shoeing job will be of great benefit to achieve this end. The shoeing regulations concerning pleasure classes for Morgans stipulate that shoes, including pads, must not exceed 4½ inches. It says further that "shoes must be plain heel shoes which follow the natural contour of the wall of the hoof, without bars and not turned in at the heels."

To find the best head position, experiment a little with your checkrein. Vary it up or down and in conjunction with different bits (if using side checks). The horse should have a relatively high head carriage and the checkrein must not hinder his free forward motion. If it is too tight his motion will be restricted, his action choppy and his attitude unhappy. If it is too loose the motion may tend to be a bit unbalanced, his head will lower, putting too much weight on his forehand and his action will be lower and erratic. The possibility of a break is greater with a loose checkrein, as is the chance of some mischief such as a playful buck or kick. As the head set is quite important in the performance of the horse, the position of the checkrein is an area that deserves considerable emphasis.

Pleasure Driving Morgan mare, "Paramounts Gigi," owned by Intrepid Farms, Carpinteria, Calif., and driven by James Wigle, a consistent winner in this class.

When asked to back up the horse should lower and flex his head as he steps backward with diagonal feet moving in unison. Using the pull and release method this is easily achieved and straightness should be maintained. Three or four steps backward will be sufficient and the horse should then walk readily—and easily—back to his original position in the line up.

Roadster Section

The Morgan Roadster should be of ideal type with perhaps a little longer neck and more height. He must not be too fine or weedy looking and should have those attributes which are the heritage of the Morgan, i.e., stamina, substance, presence, and a willing attitude. He may have slightly greater length of body to give him more ability at speed but he must retain the symmetry and proportions that so distinguish the breed.

The Roadster should display considerable animation, presence and brilliance with his action and bearing since he is closer to that of the Park Harness horse than that of the Pleasure Driving Horse.

The Morgan horse is ideally suited to his role as Roadster due to his heritage. In the early days of Morgan history, they were bred and noted for their trotting ability and indeed until around 1855 a Morgan held the trotting record of the times. Then along came the Standardbred horses—which incidentally had a lot of Morgan blood—and beginning with the great Hambletonian, shattered the existing trotting records.

The gaits called for in the Roadster class are the jog trot, road gait and the trot at speed. They are judged on performance, speed, quality and manners. Judges may ask a Roadster to back. The principal gait for roadsters is the trot and the three distinct and different speeds called for give great scope for the Morgan to demonstrate his ability across the spectrum.

The slow jog trot is similar to the slow trot of the Pleasure Driving horse but has greater animation and brilliance. Obvious presence and great controlled energy should be apparent. This gait should be true, square and deliberate and the horse should work easily without undue restraint.

Road gait is a medium fast trot performed with great animation and brilliance. Similar to the animated trot of the Park Harness horse but with a bit more speed, it is characterized by a longer stride, more fluidness of action and the feeling it conveyed of tremendous pent up speed potential. The road gait must be performed in a balanced diagonal manner with the horse working off his hocks and demonstrating form. He should be up in his bridle but light-mouthed and readily controllable. He must not anticipate the command to "drive on" and fight the bit or become otherwise excited to the detriment of way of going and cadence.

When asked to drive on, the horse should make the transition to top speed with ease and form. The transition should not be awkward or jerky and his head set ought to remain high and flexed. The trot at speed is a thrilling, exciting and crowd pleasing gait and because of this the driver must beware of getting carried away with enthusiasm and sacrificing form for speed. The horse must be made to go right into his corners with no side reining, reverse bending or loss of balance. He must never pace, break or run on the turns and should come out of the corners flat and at great speed. He should stay on the rail at all times unless it becomes necessary to pass and his driver must be very alert and aware of the positions of the other horses. A driver who turns out to pass at speed without glancing behind is likely to cause either a bad accident or an upset if another horse has turned out to pass at the same time. By the same token, when pulling back onto the rail, make certain you are not cutting off the horse behind you. The Roadsters at speed should demonstrate brilliance, clean action and precision which will be combined with keeness, beauty, and obvious enthusiasm.

Equipment

The Morgan in a Roadster class will wear a very fine and light show harness. The bridle should have square blinkers and an overdraw checkrein used in conjunction with a snaffle bit. The noseband or caveson may be of patent leather to match the browband and blinkers. The breast collar should be very fine, no more than 1½ inches wide and should be of the folded and sewn style. The traces should be sewn on and may be made round back to the flat ends if so desired. A running martingale is required, the forks of which may also be of rounded leather. The backpad should be very fine and trimmed with patent leather, and ought not to exceed 2½ inches in width. The bellyband will be of folded and sewn style with fine wrap straps. The crupper will be sewn onto the crupper strap which should not be wider than ¾ of an inch. Reins can be made round back to the hand parts and will be of show quality, preferably with steel-lined ends where buckled onto the bit. Thimbles are usually worn in a Roadster class and should be of fine quality with straps no wider than ⅝ of an inch. Brass hardware throughout is customary and buckles are sometimes covered in leather or rubber. The entire harness will likely weigh no more than 15 pounds.

Morgans in Roadster classes are shown to a bike—a light two-wheeled sulky. It usually has 26-inch heavy duty chromed wheels with wide tires mounted in forks. The driver sits on a small seat in the center with his feet up in stirrups—small supports hung from the inside of each shaft and positioned behind the crossbar. These bikes are usually made of varnished wood but many metal and fiberglass types have now made their appearance. The bike is an extremely light vehicle, generally weighing not more than forty pounds. For show ring use bikes usually feature a considerable amount of chrome, where the race track counterpart will settle for a less conspicuous finish.

The overall effect of the Roadster turnout should be beautiful, exciting and controlled speed.

Training

The slow jog trot is easily obtained from the ability our young colt has already attained with his training. He will have previously demonstrated his potential along roadster lines so we will merely have to channel his energy and activity along these lines. To achieve the slow jog trot required in the show ring we will ask for greater impulsion and animation while restraining the colt to the desired speed. The colt will be wearing an overdraw checkrein in keeping with roadster regulations and we must experiment with the length of this until we find the right height to achieve best results. A roadster generally wears a tighter checkrein than the other Morgan harness classes because it improves and steadies his balance at speed.

Make sure you drive right into the corners because a horse, young or old, soon learns to cut his corners and turn his head the opposite way. He must not side rein or cut corners. At the jog trot it is fairly easy to persuade a horse to corner easily and bend properly, but at a faster speed it becomes increasingly difficult. Encourage the colt to maintain speed and cadence throughout the turn. He should not slow down or change diagonals. This is where the earlier stages of training will show up in good balance and quick response.

The road gait follows the jog trot and is really just a faster edition of it in most ways. We cluck our horse on allowing him to stride out at greater speed but retaining strong impulsion behind. Playing our reins subtly— now squeezing, now releasing—we encourage our horse to ever greater effort making sure there is no loss of balance or form. His action should be completely fluid and easy yet high and airy.

Now we must be very careful to guide our horse around the turns properly. Do not allow him to begin side reining or hitching in the corners. If he has his balance properly established he will be able to corner in form and not skip or change stride. Any tendency to pace or rack around a corner must be severely checked at the first indication. If he does pace or rack in a show he will be instantly disqualified. Give the horse lots of support with your reins around the corners. He has to bend his body rather severely around the fairly sharp corners of a show ring, which means compressing one side while extending the other or in simple terms he has to slow down his inside side and speed up his outside side!

All the while he is accomplishing this physical feat he must also continue to trot in form with all the brilliance and animation his driver has requested. Until he learns to corner well at speed he is going to need help on every turn. Never ask your horse to take a corner faster than he is able; work up to high speed corners gradually. If you once get your horse scrambling and worrying on the corners it will be difficult to undo the damage. A roadster must always be a high-couraged animal and must therefore have great self respect. If he loses this respect and courage he will seldom be a winner in the highly competitive show ring of today.

Be sure to work your horse equally in both directions of the ring. Even after he has learned to control his gait around the corners in one direction, he will have to learn it again in the other direction. Horses are usually more adept in one direction than the other, so care must be taken to work him well in his weaker direction.

At the road gait, the horse should go boldly and with even, determined strides. He should convey the feeling that he is really going somewhere and that his road-covering stride will certainly get him there. The road gait—as the term implies—is the gait at which horses of earlier days went along performing the work of our modern automobiles.

The trot at speed is a breathtaking spectacle for the onlooker and an exhilarating thrill for the driver. At the command "drive on", the horse seems to develop into a veritable speed machine. The transition from the road gait to top speed should be almost instantaneous and absolutely smooth. These transitions must be practiced over and over, each time asking the horse for more speed until he can develop satisfactory response. He should not be pushed beyond his real capabilities, however, or his gait will become uncoordinated and rough, but he must be taught to trot increasingly faster. The best place to teach the trot at speed is out on a half mile track or any area that is flat, has good footing and nice long straight stretches. It is much easier for a horse to perfect his speed where there are no sharp corners. A quiet country road is another alternative and one that gives lots of length for the job.

Give the horse good support with your reins at the fast trot, especially while cornering. The faster a horse goes the more support he needs to maintain balance and even strides. At top speed the smallest movement of hands or weight can unbalance the horse's gait. The checkrein plays a large part as well in steadying the horse at speed. Hence the importance of the earlier work in achieving the optimum length for best performance results.

As the horses's ability to trot at speed improves, we should ask for more speed in the stretches and practice tactices for cornering. We must know exactly how much speed our horse can produce and maintain and just where the point is at which he will have to break. This intimate knowledge will allow us to show our horse with confidence and finesse. We will not have to take chances because we will know with certainty our horse's capabilities *and* his shortcomings.

As our training progresses we should subject our roadster prospect to some sound effects. The crowd usually "goes wild" when the horses are asked to drive on and the arena becomes very noisy with cheers, yells and excited clapping and foot thumping, so we must prepare our young horse. Until a horse becomes accustomed to or at least introduced to such noises the effect is apt to cause him to break or even run away. It can be a very frightening experience for a novice and one that could affect him for some time. We can have someone clap and makes noises at home as we drive and gradually work up to a comparable noise level to that of a show. Some sound effect records are available and these may be found very useful.

Rattlers may be used as a training aid for the Roadster if more action is required. The modern Roadster is expected to have good action and if this area needs improving, rattlers may be of real assistance.

Quarter boots or bell boots are usually worn on the front feet of Roadsters. The quarter boots must not be weighted in any way and if they are found to be so the horse will be disqualified. Boots such as those mentioned also tend to improve a horse's action. Quarter boots, especially by their opening and closing action, act very much like rattlers and a higher, longer stride will often result from their use. Boots also afford protection for the horse's front lower legs in case of an overreach or interference. Often at top speed, especially in the turns, a horse will step too far under himself and hit his front pastern area. This can cause leg problems later on but its immediate effect is often a change in gait of the horse as he tries to favor the smarting limb. This can cost him the class if he has been in contention to that point. The white quarter or bell boots also add a dash of color contrast to the horse. At speed the quickness of pace is emphasized by those flashing white boots. The boots worn must fit the horse!

Boots come in three sizes (small, medium, and large) and the proper size for your horse should be purchased. If too big, the boot will slide around too much at the base, i.e., at the coronet band, and they will have an awkward effect. This will not encourage speed or action as the horse will find them cumbersome and clumsy. If too small, the boot will pinch the foot and the action of the boot itself will be too restricted to accomplish anything useful.

Boots on the hind feet are not normally needed or worn. However, if during training sessions you find your horse is scalping or otherwise hitting his hind feet, a scalping boot can be worn there. However, this fault should be immediately corrected by your farrier, as scalping is usually a shoeing problem.

Justin Morgan Class

This class requires the Morgan to demonstrate his real versatility and stamina. The requirements are designed to eliminate any faint-hearted or specialized animals. Entries must trot a half mile in harness, run a half mile under saddle, show in the ring at a walk, trot and canter, and lastly pull a stone boat (500 pounds minimum total weight) a distance of 6 feet in work harness. Any horse failing to pull the stone boat the required distance is eliminated. The class is judged 25 percent on each of its four parts.

In this text we will only concern ourselves with the last requirement; i.e., the pulling event. As stated, this load is to be pulled by a Morgan wearing work harness. For the small time and distance involved it is not essential that the harness be of perfect fit but the collar should not be too far off the mark. An ill-fitting collar can cause problems over a period of time with constant use. The rule of thumb when fitting a collar is to just be able to fit the fingers of your hand between the collar and the base of the horse's neck. Width is also important as it should not pinch the neck on either side. The width of a collar is called its draught. When pulling, the traces where joined to the hames should be in line with the draught.

An ordinary work harness very often does not have blinkers so you should either supply your own bridle or be certain to accustom your horse to driving in an open bridle. The former is preferable and safer. Quite often there will be no crupper either, as this item is often unnecessary on a working harness. Checkreins are seldom used on such a harness and the backpad is wider and flatter, thus it stays put without the use of a crupper.

A horse must be taught to pull heavy loads. It is altogether different for your horse to pull a light cart or show buggy with passengers than to pull a

Roadster, Morgan horse. "Jesta Venture" (Applevale Wayfarer x Indian Lady). Many times Champion, this classic nine-year-old stallion is owned by Mr. & Mrs. Philip DuBois, Peterborough, New Hampshire and trained and driven by Peter Morin.

dead heavy weight—and on runners not wheels! The buggy and passengers would weight perhaps 450 pounds *but* it moves on wheels, making it an easy chore for any horse to move along. The 500 pound loaded stone boat is on skids or runners and the initial start is the most difficult part, because it has so much inertia and friction. The horse must lean into his collar and get right down to his work with deliberate and powerful thrusts from his hind quarters. He should *not* charge into his collar, head up, with frenzied bounds, "gee–ing and haw–ing" back and forth in his attempts to move the load. Even a 500 pound dead weight is really not all that difficult for a strong and well conditioned horse to pull, and this erratic display will undoubtedly move the load the required distance, but it points out the obvious lack of preparation given the horse.

To prepare your well-trained driving horse for this pulling event is not a difficult task at all, and both you and your horse will enjoy the new challenge. Begin by fitting the work harness. As mentioned earlier, you ought to be able to insert the four fingers of your hand between the base of the collar and the horse's neck. The hames must fit the collar, whatever type you are using. They should fit snugly in the groove and fasten top and bottom with ease. These little leathers fastening the hames are called hame straps and are extremely useful around the tack room. The backpad and bellyband on a work harness are left fairly loose; the pull on the traces (which buckle to the jockey) help keep the pad in place. A crupper may be used and the crupper strap will support the trace carriers. Your ordinary driving bridle completes the harness.

Start your horse pulling fairly light loads—first of all, an empty stone boat. This will be a different sensation for the horse as there are no shafts. Because there are no shafts it is wise to use trace carriers at first in case the horse gets a leg over a trace. To use trace carriers we must have either a crupper strap and crupper or team type breeching with the stability to support the hip strap. Horses become quite adept at stepping over and back into traces, but the first time it happens it may frighten him and a tangled mess can result. (I once ended up with a filly *sitting in* the stone boat, completely immobilized by the traces twisted round and round). The noise of the dragging stone boat is often a bit disconcerting the first few moments so you must reassure your horse with voice and attitude. Very soon he will ignore the noise and become accustomed to the traces slapping his quarters and legs.

Gradually increase the load, making sure that your horse is pulling properly. He should lower his head slightly and put his weight into the collar, hindquarters digging in and propelling him along. His pace should be slow and easy. Any inclination to rush or canter or pull out sideways must be discouraged. A horse can hurt himself lunging and slamming into the harness in an unco-ordinated and uneducated manner.

Before very long you will have your horse pulling 500 pounds with no difficulty. Practice calm starts—this is the key to a successful pull. Teach your horse to use his weight and momentum to do the initial work, rather than acting like a battering ram or a catapult.

Be careful not to overdo the pulling business. Despite his muscular build and ability he is not a draft horse and too much heavy work could cause damage to muscles and tissues. Do only enough pulling to teach your horse how to do it properly and to accustom him to the equipment used in the class.

Within image: "DYBERRY ROBIN" Justin Morgan Class PACIFIC NORTHWEST MORGAN SHOW Walla Walla June 14, 1969 Showman Dr. Elmer Searls Owners Dr. & Mrs. Elmer Searls

Justin Morgan Class. "Dyberry Robin" Morgan stallion. Owned and driven by Dr. Elmer Searls, Puyallup, Washington

Gay 90s Class (sometimes called Cavalcade Americana)

This colorful class is not an AHSA or CHSA class and the specifications can vary from show to show depending upon the show committee who draw up the rules. Generally, the requirements are as follows: two or more persons to ride in a two or four-wheeled vehicle drawn by one or more horses. Vehicles and costumes should be typical of those used prior to 1900 and displayed at a walk, trot or extended trot. The class is judged on performance, manners and conformation (60%) and type and appointments (40%). Some show committees specify that the occupants should be a gentleman and a lady, either to drive, but other shows leave the driver and passengers up to the entrant.

In any case, the vehicles should be authentic and if restored, true to its original shape. As many original fittings and pieces should be preserved and used in restoring an old vehicle as is possible. The costumes of the passengers should also be as authentic as possible and should match the vehicle in which they are riding, i.e., a sedate and formal type of vehicle should not be ridiculed by passengers wearing funny, frivolous or picnic-type attire.

This class gives wonderful scope to the Morgan breed to demonstrate its history. Gigs, buckboards, surreys, doctor's buggies and countless others all played a part in our early history and more than often a Morgan horse was pulling them. History can be replayed as these vehicles are driven correctly appointed in the Gay 90s class. Single horses, teams, tandems and four-in-hands can all be used with various vehicles to recreate scenes of yore—with the entrants enjoying the class as much as the spectators.

At some shows it is customary for the entrants to give a written description of the vehicle he is entering which can be read out during the class and which adds more understanding and enjoyment for everyone. With these old-fashioned vehicles having become so hard to obtain, it is rare for spectators to have the opportunity to see such a number at one time. The description and pertinent data are of great interest.

The gaits called for are the same as the Pleasure Driving Class and are performed and judged in the same way. The harness will differ with the vehicle, as heavier type carriages need equally heavier harness. This is very important: the harness must be in keeping with the vehicle both in weight, strength and design. Some of the heavier vehicles will necessitate a collar and hames and these must be of a type suitable for the vehicle. A work horse type of harness would look terribly out of place drawing a fancy Victoria or Landau, while if the vehicle was a farm wagon of a hundred years ago, the fine patent leather collars and brass hames of the showy harness would be ridiculous. When using collar and hames, a perfect fit must be achieved, otherwise damage can be done to the horse in short order.

No special training is necessary for this class, except to ensure that the horse or horses are well accustomed to pulling the particular vehicle to be used.

Gay 90s Morgan Class. "Beckridge Oraette," #012470, Morgan mare owned by Mr. and Mrs. Leo Beckley, Beckridge Farms, Mount Vernon, Washington and driven by Mr. Tom Bradshaw.

4
THE HACKNEY HORSE

The spirited, high-stepping Hackney has been around for a long time. The word "Hackney" derives from the Norman–French word "Hac-

Hackney horse to a Gig. "Marden Striplight," owned and driven by Mr. George D. Newman, St. Catharines, Ontario with Mr. John McCaughey, the footman, shown to a Stanhope Gig. Undefeated in 1975 and 1976, he was also chosen "All-American Gig Horse."

quene" which refers to a type of riding horse used around 1250. The Hackney originated from the Norfolk Trotter and the Godolphin Arabian. With a trotting background that has its foundation in ancient history it is no wonder that the Hackney is a trotting specialist!

Around the nineteenth century in England the improvement in roads and surfaces led to development of both the sport of driving and the carriage makers' art. Hard, good surfaces gave an incentive for the use of elegant carriages and highly bred horses, in particular the Hackney horse.

The Hackney is noted for his magnificent and breathtaking high action, both front and rear. It is very important that the hock action be powerful and true, they must truly "pop" their hocks. It is not without reason that Hackneys are called "The Peacocks of the Show Ring". They possess high, proud head carriage, elegant snappy action, rythmic true cadence, and above all, a presence that just shouts "Look at me!"

Hackneys are noted for their soundness and disposition as well as their distinctive action. It is very rare to find a splint or leg ailment on a Hackney.

The first English Hackney imported to this country was the stallion Bellfounder (Mr. Jary's). This celebrated horse was a beautiful bright bay 7 years old standing 15 hands high. He was allowed by the best judges in Norfolk to be the fastest and best bred horse ever sent out of that country and his superior blood, symmetry and action excelled over every other trotting stallion of that time. His importation in 1822 paved the way for subsequent Hackney imports, all bearing impeccable pedigrees and thus began the tremendous popularity of this breed.

The classes, equipment and training for Hackney horses are the same as that of the Hackney Pony and are covered in detail in the next chapter.

Pair Hackney horses. "Suddie Marshal" and "Marden Striplight" shown to a Basket Phaeton. Owned and driven by Mr. George D. Newman, St. Catharines, Ontario with Mr. John McCaughey the footman. This pair won the open pair class at Syracuse, Ottawa, and the Royal Winter Fair in 1976 and were "All-American Pair" for that year.

Tandem of Hackney horses. "Marden Striplight" wheeler, and "Suddie Marshal," leader, winning the tandem class at the 1976 Royal Winter Fair. Owned and driven by George D. Newman of St. Catharines, Ontario with Mr. John McCaughey, footman.

5
THE HACKNEY PONY

The Hackney pony evolved from the Hackney horse. In the year 1872 scientific breeding to fix the pony type within the breed was begun in England. The foundation sire of the pony was a 14-hand brown Yorkshire-bred Hackney stallion named Sir George. In 1883 when the Hackney Horse Society was established in England, the dividing line between horse and pony became clearly defined.

The first Hackney Pony to be imported into the United States was Stella in the year 1878. In 1898 came the beautiful brown pony stallion Dilham Prime Minister 743 and in 1903 the famous Enfield Nipper 640. These two stallions may be considered the most important foundation sires of the modern American Hackney pony.

Hackney ponies exhibit the same magnificent high and snappy action as the Hackney Horses, but with their smaller stature, fineness and proud bearing, these little fellows appear to be going much higher and livelier than their large counterparts. Their fiery spirited way of going—determination coupled with elegance, their fantastic show ring presence and their pleasing conformation and size make them one of the major attractions at any show. Their disposition is usually excellent, calm, and tractable, they are willing and ever ready to work and are easily kept.

Hackney ponies are shown in harness in several classes: single hackney pony; hackney pony gig class; single hackney pony ladies, junior exhibitors, amateurs owners; pair of hackney ponies; pair ladies or amateur; tandem hackney ponies; collection of three ponies and four-in-hands. Each class is to be shown at special gaits and is judged on slightly different considerations. We will go into specific detail as we discuss each indivdual class.

Hackney ponies are to be exhibited with a short mane braided and short tail. In all classes tradition suggests the following appointments:

apron, gloves and whip. Excessive speed is neither required nor expected.

For horse show purposes the maximum height of Hackney ponies is 14:2 hands. Classes may be divided: 13 hands and under, over 13 hands and not exceeding 14:2 hands. In pair classes a difference of one-half inch in the height of the two ponies is allowable without penalty. If the difference exceeds one-half inch it will count against the entry.

One attendant is permitted to stand inside the gate while a class is in progress and only one attendant is allowed to head a pony. Ponies may be unchecked while lined up except in Ladies, Junior Exhibitors, Amateur and Owner classes.

Shoeing

The Hackney has inherited a good foot and the breed has an excellent reputation for soundness. Hackney ponies are usually shown with fairly long feet, pads and varying weights of shoes. It is not uncommon to see ponies with 4-inch toes. The important thing is to keep the natural angle of the pony's foot. Even though the toe and heel are both quite long, the natural angle of the foot is almost unchanged and the tendons are not being strained in any way. One only has to look at all the sound ponies showing with these long feet and see them performing happily to realize that they are certainly not uncomfortable in the hoof department.

Past a certain length, however, the angle the foot makes with the ground must be made slightly steeper or strain could result. As heels are more difficult to grow than toes, the farrier sometimes will use a wedge-shaped pad to make up the added length needed to obtain the necessary angle. To keep feet healthy at this unnatural length, the foot must be well packed with some hoof preparation (or the good old pine tar and oakum of yesteryear) to keep it moist. Leather or rubber pads are then put on and lastly the shoe. If lead needs to be added for more action or balance it is often put under the pad and attached to the pad. These pads are quite thick and protect the sole of the foot as well as keep in the moisture.

The shoe itself takes many forms depending on the pony's way of going, any overreaching problems, need for higher action or longer stride. What form the shoe takes is best left to your farrier, who should be qualified to correct any problems and to shoe the pony for the job he has to do. One condition that must be guarded against is contracted heels or heels that become too narrow. Frequency of shoeing depends upon the growth rate of the foot, surface travelled and the type of hoof—whether firm rubbery hoofs that hold nails well or brittle chalky hooves that are difficult to keep nails in. Some ponies are shod only every two months, while other have to be reset every six or even four weeks. Time can never be the sole factor with so many other variables.

There is no limit to length or weight as far as hackney regulations are concerned, but both length and weight are self limiting in the fact that the pony can only carry so much of both without losing style, form and animation.

In the event of the pony throwing a shoe during a class, the judging is suspended for a period of not more than seven minutes to allow the pony to be reshod. No animal is permitted more than one such exemption in a given class. The seven minutes also supplies to repairs to broken equipment.

Braiding

Hackney ponies are shown braided except in Gig classes where they are shown with unbraided manes.

When manes are braided finely and neatly the pony's neck is enhanced and the whole turnout looks neater. The added color of the yarn gives more showiness to the turnout. Any color yarn may be used to braid and some drivers match the color to the shade of clothing or apron worn. Some colors go better than others with a particular color of pony.

Usually the bridle path on a hackney pony is shaved with electric clippers back perhaps 3 to 4 inches. This enhances the lines of the pony's neck and throat as well as making a clean area for the crown of the bridle. Long bridle paths are unnecessary and do not improve things as a rule.

While on the subject of shaving with electric clippers it is of interest to note that trainers usually shave the whiskers off the pony, shave under his jowl and chin, shave off his eye lashes (the reason for this is so that they will not hit the blinkers and cause the pony to fuss or shake his head) and also shave inside and around the pony's ears. Naturally all this has to be done tactfully and kindly. If patience is shown the pony will seldom need a twitch or artificial restraint. It is also usual to shave off all but a small amount of forelock as only one braid is desired and too much hair will make it bulky and thick. It is also regular practice to shave the pony's pasterns and around the coronet band area to make it clean and tidy. Excess hair is also shaved off the fetlocks and white stockings are completely shaved.

Thick or heavy yarn is easier to use when braiding, but several strands of fine yarn may be used if necessary. Yarn is usually cut into 18 to 20 inch lengths and it is wise to cut it well in advance of the time for actual braiding. Some prefer to stand on a small stool or box to braid the mane, or if tall enough one can braid from the ground on most ponies. The mane ought to be well brushed and combed out before starting to braid to facilitate easy braiding. The mane is usually pulled or cut off in some manner to a fairly short length, about 4 inches to prevent too bulky or thick braids.

Lay the cut yarn across the pony's back and starting at the right side of the mane, i.e., nearest the ears, part the hair into about a half inch or whatever you wish with your comb. Braid down to within about two inches of the end of the hair, then pick up a strand of yarn and holding it by the middle, braid it into the hair for the remainder of the length of hair. Tie the hair and yarn together into a tight knot and leave. Part the next width of hair and repeat the procedure. Keep repeating these little braids all the way down the mane to the withers, usually about twenty braids. Now go around to the left side and with a bent wire, a pair of surgical "mosquito clamps" or similar device reach through the base of the braid right on the neck, and pull the end of the braid through. Pull it through until the required length is achieved, doubled over—about 1 inch. Go down the mane pulling all the braids through before starting to tie them.

Next, starting at one end, proceed to tie the yarn around and around the doubled braid near the neck edge, then knot it leaving about 1½ to 2 inches of loose yarn. Do this all they way to the end. Then take scissors and trim all the way up the mane, snipping off excess yarn and making an even job of the loose ends. More yarn can be added if it appears too thin in any place. The main thing is to have it regular, even and straight up the neck, not zigzagging left and right in little S–curves! Don't forget to include the forelock in your braiding. It is done the same way as the mane—just one little braid—with the ends of the yarn snipped off.

After a class, the sooner the braids are taken out, the easier the job will be and the least mess of waves and tangles will result. Braids can be left in overnight for a two day show, but they are usually rather untidy by the second day. It is best to braid each day. With practice and the right kind of yarn, the job can be done in under an hour. The job is best done with the pony on cross-ties. This keeps his head more or less in place, as any movement really messes up the braiding. After several braidings the pony usually learns to stand very still, and becomes used to the process. If possible, the pony should not be braided until an hour or so before his class, as he is usually kept on the cross-ties until his class is called and he may get very restless and cramped if left for several hours.

Hackneys are never "worked down" before a class as are some other breeds; on the contrary they are usually ground driven just enough to loosen them up and work them up a little before entering the ring. Some are just taken straight out of their stalls, hitched and driven right into the ring. The first five or ten minutes of a hackney's performance are probably the most brilliant and animated, and the maximum degree of high spirit and stored up energy is desired.

Tails

Hackney ponies are shown as cob tails, which usually means that they have been docked. Docks are done in varying lengths, the average about five inches. A trend lately is toward the "Canadian Cut", which merely involves cutting the tail hair off at the end of the tail bone looking like a very long dock. This is perhaps more humane as it gives the pony a bit of a flyswatter.

The tails are worn almost straight up on a slight backward angle and are supported in spoon cruppers or a tail brace. It has become common practice lately to wear hoods on their tails, a false tail in other words, which is laced on over the real tail and the spoon of the crupper. But a pony sporting a good amount of natural tail hair has no need of this artificial equipment.

Before one can put a pony's tail in a high crupper, the pony must be brought gradually up to this point with either a tail set or a bustle (an oversize fat crupper). He must become accustomed to having his tail in this unnatural position and the muscles must also be taught to accept the fact. The surface of these high cruppers must be kept extremely clean and free of any grime or the pony will very quickly develop a sore tail. For the first few times, a pad of cotton batting will help to prevent any soreness and fear of the crupper. A pony can develop a very genuine dislike and fear of the high crupper if it makes him sore a few times. Kicking out backwards is one of the results that can occur from misuse of this piece of equipment.

Bitting

Hackneys are shown in Liverpool bits, Buxton bits, and other elbow style curb bits. They are used in conjunction with a small check bit of either jointed or straight type. The most common bit used is the Liverpool, and the most widely used position with this bit is the half cheek, or rough cheek as it is sometimes called. For Ladies or Amateur classes it is mandatory for the pony to be driven in the half cheek position.

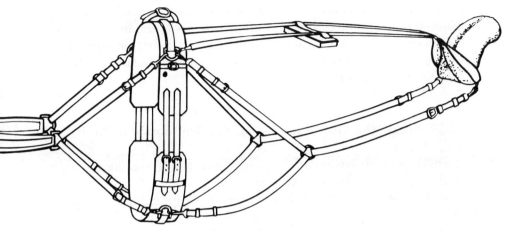

Tail Set.

There are four positions in which the reins can be attached when using a Liverpool bit. The open cheek position on the ring gives no curb action at all, the half cheek position a slight amount of curb, and the lower two positions give increasingly severe curb action.

Liverpool bits come with either fixed or swivel cheeks, and some ponies will work better in one style than the other. Whichever style is used, you must make sure the bit is wide enough—about half an inch wider than the pony's mouth. When using the fixed cheek type of Liverpool, it is wise to bend outward slightly the upper part of the cheeks (the part above the bit) so that it does not press too tightly against the pony's cheeks.

The Liverpool is used with a curb chain which should be twisted until all the links lie flat in the curb groove under his chin. It should not be too tight, rather adjusted so that the cheek pieces can be pulled back to a 45° angle. A leather curb strap with chain links at either end is often more acceptable to a pony. Keep in mind that you can exert a tremendous amount of leverage with the reins, especially as the pony is already wearing a tight-fitting noseband. Use your curb sparingly.

Checkreins

Hackneys are always shown in side checks, overdraw checkreins are not permitted. A piece of equipment that is usually used where overdraw style checkreins are used is the running martingale, which is seldom seen with side checks or on hackney ponies. Side checks can be of two styles: the running bridoon or direct type. The latter is the most common on ponies. This type is now mostly made of nylon sash cord but used to be made of round leather. The checkrein attaches to the bridoon either by french snaps or buckles, runs through drops on the crown piece and part way down the neck from which is attached a short adjustable leather piece with the tab for the backpad hook.

Single Hackney Pony (open, maiden, novice or limit)

This class is shown at Park Pace and Show Your Pony, and is judged on quality, performance and manners.

Park Pace is a smart trot showing great animation, high well cadenced

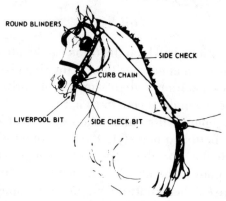

Side Checks.

action with great elegance and spirit, powerful hock action and true diagonal strides. "Show your pony" means exactly what it says—show your pony to its best ability. Usually this means a slightly faster speed to bring out the very best of everything, but it is seldom seen to be greatly different from the Park Pace.

Both gaits are shown both ways of the ring and both feature a very high head carriage. High knee action coupled with well folded lower legs is the classic distinctive style recognized by even the uninitiated. A cheerful and willing attitude should be apparent and he must work with tremendous animation. There should be no head throwing, fighting the bit, tail switching or roaring.

As quality is the first consideration, the pony should have good conformation. To perform with top action he must have a good sloping shoulder and his neck and head should come well up out of his wither. He should have strong and supple muscle structure, a compact body and powerful quarters. He ought to be short in the back, have powerful loins, lots of room in the chest, not too short in the neck (although a hackney does not have the long neck of some other breeds) and a small, rather straight head. He has full prominent eyes set wide apart and small well-shaped ears. Of all breeds, he has to my mind the most alert and expressive ears. They are always on the move, listening, talking, and telegraphing thoughts. The hackney's thighs and quarters are well muscled and the pasterns of good length and slope.

Since performance is the second consideration, the pony should give of his very best and display that magnificent and breathtaking high action for which he is famous. His trot must be a truly diagonal gait, his front legs lifting airily with the "hackney snap" so unique to this breed, while the hind legs develop tremendous power and animation. The hocks must exhibit good action as well as the front knees, and as all front action depends upon the amount of impulsion from the back, the hind end is most important. The Hackney must have above all else great animation and presence because a top performance hinges on these.

The third consideration is manners, which the pony should display on both the rail and in the line up. He should not have sour ears, show balkiness, unwillingness, animosity toward the other ponies, fight the bit, pull over much, or display any kicking tendencies. He should work cheerfully, with alert ears and willingly obey the instructions of his driver. He should not roar, whistle, or exhibit other signs of choking down. His manners should be such as to impress and please the ordinary onlooker and in this way promote the breed. Although another hackney owner or capable trainer might enjoy seeing a fiery, unruly and almost unmanageable pony being driven, the ordinary person would be completely put off the whole breed by such a display. Manners are important in any class and with any breed, but the aristocratic little Hackney pony must show really good manners to uphold his heritage.

Equipment

The harness required in this class is the same for all hackney pony classes except gig classes and team classes when shown to a Viceroy show buggy.

The bridle, of course, is extremely fine, both because of its style and its small size. It has the ordinary compliments plus round blinkers, side checks, face drop and usually a Liverpool bit. It has flat cheeks, patent leather browband with chain decoration across the width, patent leather blinkers and often patent leather noseband. The face drop is usually of patent leather, too. This face drop is purely decorative and has no other purpose. It buckles onto the little buckle in the center of the crown piece and hangs down the horse's face under the browband. It is usual to have a separate check bit with a hackney bridle, and it can be either jointed or straight according to preference.

The breast collar is very fine, no wider than 1¼ inches, and is folded and sewn with raised patent leather trim. The traces are the buckled on type and are sometimes made round or beaded for more style. The breast collar is supported by a very fine neck strap with hold back tab; the neck strap is often made round.

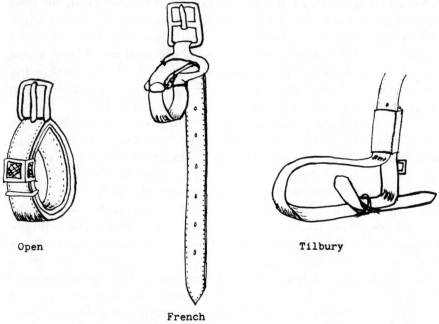

Open

French

Tilbury

Various types of shaft loops.

The backpad is patent leather all around and well padded. The most modern ones are mounted on the new spring steel trees, and its bellyband has folded and sewn style with patent leather raised layer. Sometimes a piece of heavy elastic is let into the center of the bellyband and will be more comfortable for some ponies. The shaft loops on hackney harness are usually of french style or sometimes tilbury style. It is interesting to note that when using this style of shaft loop, it is done up much tighter than when using open loops and wrap straps. There are no wrap straps

with french or tilbury loops, so they must be tighter to do their job. The
crupper strap (or back strap) is usually narrow, about ½ inch, and has
buckled on crupper. The crupper can be of several types: ordinary, spoon
or stand up style, all of which buckle on and are interchangeable.
Breeching is not worn, nor are thimbles. All hardware is of solid brass.
Reins are either all tan and beaded or narrow black front parts with tan
hand parts. It is also correct to use round russett reins. Most reins have
steel ends at the buckle.

The vehicle used by Hackney ponies in this class and most classes is
the Viceroy. The Viceroy show buggy is a fancy little four-wheeled
vehicle with an upside down "U" appearance in the seat area. Seating just
one person, it is an extremely elegant buggy, trimmed with large amounts
of chrome and patent leather. Its distinctive appearance matches the
distinctive gait of its motive power—the Hackney pony!

*Hackney pony to a Viceroy. "Silver Creek Party Girl," Champion
Hackney Pony mare, owned and driven by Mrs. R. N. Miller, Bend,
Oregon. Oregon State Champion Hackney Pony for 1975.*

Training

The early stages of training for a Hackney pony are not very different from those used for all other breeds (which have already been thoroughly covered.) The pony is taught to wear the harness step by step, then lunged with it, and finally driven on the reins from the ground. Here the difference begins. A Hackney is given much more ground driving than other breeds. It is from this beginning that much of his future action and form will derive. The pony is taught to go up into his bridle and to put out greater and greater amounts of impulsion which is channeled into action rather than speed. The trainer runs either well behind or out to one side as he drives the pony, or often drives from a central point in the middle of the training ring using very long lines. By judicious use of the whip as the pony trots around the ring on long lines, snapping and cracking it in conjunction with voice commands and clucks (but not touching the pony with it as a rule), the pony is worked up to a high degree of collection and animation. His cadence is also perfected in this way, and his head is gradually brought up with the checkreins until it is in the position desired by his trainer.

The use of a training or bitting rig or harness will be found to have a lot of value in the early stages of schooling. This can be used particularly on cold or wet days when it is unsuitable to work outdoors or just to let the pony exercise by himself in his stall.

The harness consists of a body roller, crupper, and side reins. The body roller should be well padded and have several rings at various heights to which the side reins will attach. The crupper should be padded with sheepskin or some similar cushioning material as the pony will wear the harness for periods of an hour or more in his stall and could make his tail sore. A mouthing bit, preferably of copper, is snapped onto the halter and the side reins attached. These side reins are just tight enough to make the pony give slightly with his chin. As he walks around his stall wearing this rig, he can eat and be comfortable, but is invited to flex slightly by the action of the elastic side reins. Chain rattlers or any type rattler can be put on at the same time, thus accomplishing several things at once. He also gets considerable exercise walking around with this rig.

The training harness can be left on for an hour or more with good results providing the side reins are not too tight. The pony should be checked periodically to make sure everything is all right and he is not have any problem. If the side reins are too tight or left on for very long, the pony's mouth will be rubbed raw and the training effect of no value. Instead of becoming accustomed to the bit and learning to give to it, the pony will be afraid and resentful of having it in his mouth. Care must be shown to ensure that the bit is the right size for the pony's mouth and not too narrow.

While on the subject of the pony's mouth, make sure that you have your veterinarian check the pony's teeth at least once a year. Many habits and faults are wrongly blamed on the bit when it has been caused by a tooth problem. Horses' teeth can often become very sharp and cut the animal's tongue, especially with a bit in his mouth. Wolf teeth, too, can be a big problem. These teeth are usually right where the bit sits in the horse's mouth, often just under the surface and very sharp. It is excruciatingly painful for the horse to have a severe bit or hard hands on the bit pulling on his mouth right over these teeth. Wolf teeth should be pulled as soon as discovered because they cause nothing but trouble.

As his training advances and his head set improves, a dumb jockey may be of considerable value. The checkrein is attached to the rings of the dumb jock at whatever height is desired. The crupper strap must be moved at the same time to hold back at this point of attachment. This forces the pony to carry his head and neck in a much more elevated and flexed manner and must *not* be overdone. The pony can be left in his stall in the dumb jock for twenty minutes or lunged in the ring and made to really use his hocks and work in a greatly animated fashion.

Action aids such as wooden or chain rattler are also used at this stage of training. They greatly enhance the action produced by the pony when used in conjunction with the whip and voice as discussed earlier. There are other ways to achieve action—by means of pulleys, elastics and "W" type devices—but they require expert and detailed special instruction and administration beyond the scope of this book.

After a suitable amount of time, such as when the pony is driving from the ground with good action, animation, balance and obedience, the trainer considers him ready to hitch in the two-wheeled cart. Unless the pony is terribly obstreperous or hard to control, poles are seldom used in the training of Hackney ponies. They seem to be born to the cart and take to it readily with few preliminaries.

The pony is first shown the cart. While someone pulls it around a while, the trainer drives the horse from the ground. This is normally enough to assure a good start. A safety line should nevertheless be put on the pony. This is accomplished by the helper holding the pony while the driver hitches him in the shafts of the cart. The shafts are drawn up over the top and let down on each side of the pony, never pulled straight forward because the pony would be jabbed if he moved sideways. Traces

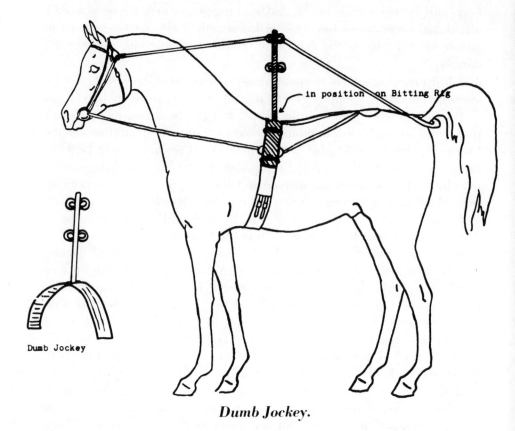

— in position on Bitting Rig

Dumb Jockey

Dumb Jockey.

are put on and wrap straps done up snugly—the shafts should not bounce up and down on the pony. With the checkrein put on (fairly long the first time to allow the pony to gain his balance in the cart), the driver picks up the reins.

The helper should assist by leading off the pony while the driver walks beside the cart driving the pony. The pony derives a good deal of confidence from the presence of the helper who is also in a position to assist the driver should the pony act up or refuse to go forward.

After a few rounds of the ring the direction is reversed and a few more trips around the ring are made with the helper still on the safety line, but not leading the pony. If everything then looks under control, the driver may get into the cart and after a round or two dispense with the safety line. The pony is walked both ways of the ring at his animated walk or allowed to trot slowly if he prefers to go at this gait. He is then gradually asked to move on at the gaits previously practiced on the long lines from the ground.

Most of the work of a Hackney pony is done on the rail; seldom are they worked in circles and figures as are the other breeds. It is wise to do some of these, however, to achieve good flexing, bending and balance. If in a ladies driver class, for instance, one is asked to drive a figure eight at a park pace, the pony must be able to do so with good form and balance, not all sprawled out or scrambling on the short turns.

The reverse is a requirement that is often badly abused. It is not correct in a harness class to turn around in a small circle! This is the accepted way under saddle, but with a cart or buggy attached it is neither suitable nor feasable—and looks dreadful. When the reverse is called for, the driver achieves the new direction by going across the ring on a diagonal and changing direction as he enters the track. This makes both the beginning and the end of the reverse a fluid and graceful turn and shows the pony and vehicle to best advantage. It is a pretty sight to see a class of good drivers reversing from both ends of the ring and passing each other in the center with nary a problem or awkward moment. When crossing the ring the line ought to be straight, not slewing and S–curving all over the arena. It should be accomplished with decisiveness and promptness. One thing to remember when meeting another pony and vehicle head on, such as in the centre of the diagonal: the rule of the ring is to keep to *your* own right! If you remember this, there should be no worry about running into someone during the reverse maneuver.

A bitting rig is used a great deal in the continued training of Hackney ponies and especially in conjunction with a dumb jockey. The bitting rig helps set the head and encourage flexing of the poll and neck as well as "give" to the bit. The dumb jockey gives more agility to the settings of the rig. The dumb jockey itself is a pole or upright piece secured to the top center of the backpad of the bitting rig. It bears rings at several levels to which the side checks, side reins and crupper strap may be attached. This elevates the controls and promotes better head carriages in some cases, and as a fringe benefit, higher action. It also tends to make a pony use his hind end to a greater degree by shifting the balance or center of gravity. The pony can be lunged or driven with the bitting rig or dumb jockey, thus teaching him to bend and flex under conditions similar to actual work.

Draw reins are also often used in the training of Hackneys, but must be used with great care and light hands. The rein is buckled onto the dee on the backpad, run through the bit ring, back through the rein terret and hence to the driver's hands. This can achieve a really good flex on a pony, but must not be kept up for too long a period nor used with the utmost leverage possible, or the mouth of the pony will suffer greatly.

The pony must be taught to line up properly and stand in line in a slightly stretched position. The helper assists in the beginning but after awhile the pony learns that when he is stopped in lineup position he should stretch. A shake of the lines will cause him to set himself up without help. To start with, the pony is stopped in the center of the ring and made to stand still; he must learn to stand still and not fidget. The helper then causes him to stretch either by tapping his front legs or manually lifting them out into position. As the driver shakes the lines he may say "stretch" or use some other signal that may be understood by the pony after much association. Make a fuss over the pony when he does stand and stretch and soon he will try for the praise and stretch on his own. Do not be in a hurry to teach the pony to back up. Let him learn to go forward well and to stand still and stretch first.

When he is really good at this level, then the back up can be taught. It should be taught from the ground first without being hitched. He then should be asked to back while being ground driven using the pull and release method, achieving one step at a time and always in control. When you are certain that he understands the command you can ask for it in the cart, but initially have him back up just the empty cart with you on the ground so that it is fairly easy for him. After a few steps in reverse, always ask him to walk forward to where he originally stood and set himself up again. When stretched, always make sure his hind feet are together, not one in front and one behind. They should be even. When he will back the empty cart with ease, then the driver may get in and ask for the back up. One thing to remember in lineup before backing your pony is to walk him forward one step to get out of his stretch before asking him to back up. It is very difficult for him to back up directly out of a stretched position and also unsightly and awkward.

It is wise to accustom the pony to periods of standing in line, set up with his head checked up. Occasionally in the lineup he will be allowed to be unchecked by the header for a few moments while the judge is not looking at him, but for the majority of the time he will be expected to stand quietly and unresistingly in the checked up position.

Start with the check fairly loose so that it is not too much strain on his muscles or patience, and make him stand for a few minutes. Then move off and work a bit. Next time ask him to stand a little longer with the check still in the same position so he becomes completely accustomed to the idea. Over a period of time, gradually raise the checkrein hole by hole, making him stand quietly and without fussing. Practice the back up with check on in each position as well because he must be able to do this with his check on. Before long the pony will be able to stand in the lineup with head in the highest position required for showing him and will not fight the bit or turn his head from side to side to avoid the pull. Except in ladies, junior, and amateur classes, the pony is allowed to be unchecked for a few moments, and if he wears a very high check this is a great relief and rest for his muscles. In ladies classes, it is sometimes necessary to check the pony a bit lower to allow for the long standing period and prevent any undue fidgeting.

Once the pony is going satisfactorily in the cart he can be hitched in the Viceroy occasionally to both accustom him to it and insure against any problems when hitched to it in the show ring. If the footing in the show ring is at all heavy, the Viceroy will pull heavier than the two-wheeler he is used to, so the pony will have to work much harder to pull the show buggy. In order to retain animation and brilliance while pulling the heavier load, he ought to be worked in similar circumstances at home for a few days to build up muscles for the job and to become accustomed to the heavier vehicle. It is hard to obtain a peak performance in a heavy vehicle if the pony has never before encountered the problem.

From this point on, the pony only needs steady workouts and considerable practice. He should not be overworked or he will lose some of his keenness. Twenty minutes a day is often sufficient for a fully trained pony. Work in rattlers and with voice encouragements while restraining him will produce more action and animation. With a proper head set he need only build up muscling and condition to be ready (and stay ready) for the show ring. Conditioning, of course, includes feeding as well as work and it will be presumed that the pony's diet is one that puts him in peak health and bloom. Another facet of conditioning is grooming, and an hour of grooming daily will do wonders for your pony's coat and appearance.

Single Hackney Pony (Ladies, Junior Exhibitors, Amateurs, Owners)

This class is shown at a park pace and not faster. The rule further states that the pony should show all around action at the park pace. The class is judged on manners, quality and performance in that order of importance. Loops are not allowed in this class (hand holds).

This class is to be driven in the half cheek position on the Liverpool bit, appear to have a perfect mouth, should stand quietly and back readily. Ponies must remain check up while lined up except during a workout.

The gaits have already been discussed in the previous section and remain the same for all hackney classes, and the difference in judging is

BITTING ARRANGEMENTS — HACKNEYS

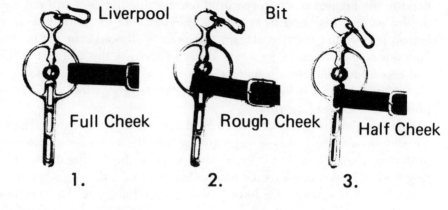

Liverpool Bit

Full Cheek   Rough Cheek   Half Cheek

1.   2.   3.

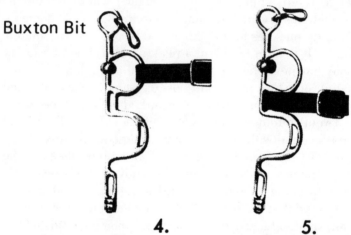

Buxton Bit

4.   5.

Bit Numbers 1, 2, 3, 4 and 5 are eligible for Lady's, Amateurs and Junior Exhibitor classes

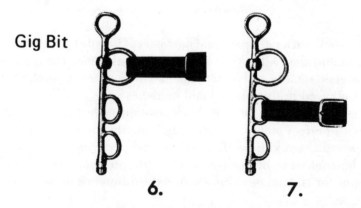

Gig Bit

6.   7.

Bit numbers 4, 5, 6 and 7 are eligible for Gig classes

Bitting positions of a Liverpool bit. (Picture Courtesy N.E.F.C.)

in the order of importance of the requirements. Since manners are the first consideration, they become of prime importance and more attention must be paid to this qualification.

Harness and vehicle are the same as in the previous section, and although this is not an appointment class, the normal traditional appointments are considered almost mandatory, i.e., apron, gloves and whip. A hat in ladies classes is often a desirable assett to completing the costume of the 'lady'.

Single Hackney Pony, open.

This class is to be shown at park pace and show your pony and is judged on performance, quality and manners.

Except for the order of importance of requirements, this class is harnessed, equipped and driven the same as the single Hackney pony, maiden, novice, or limit.

Hackney Pony Gig Class

This class is very colorful and one that has considerable spectator appeal. The gig pony or horse should be one of the most attractive of all harness horses with excellent overall conformation, action, and quality. He should be able to go at a good pace and yet have enough substance to pull a standard gig and its occupants.

The pony is shown at a walk, park pace, and smart trot and of course to a gig. The class is judged on presence, manners, quality, and performance.

The Hackney pony gig class entry *must* be driven by an amateur and ponies *must* be asked to back. Ponies also must be shown with a standing martingale.

Park pace has already been discussed, and a smart trot is just what it says: a smart trot! It is slightly faster than the park pace but retains style, form and animation.

The walk of the hackney pony is very distinctive. He throws his front legs well before him and his back ones right under his body in a style that makes his stride enormous. The hock action is very obvious at the walk, more so if it derives from good breeding rather than heavy shoes. The walk should be animated, elevated, and a definite four beat. It must never be sluggish, flat footed or dull—there must be retention of presence, style, and dignity.

Manners, quality, and performance have already been discussed but in the gig class the added requirement—the one of utmost importance—is presence. Presence is that undefinable quality that makes an individual stand out in a crowd or if alone, fairly shouts "look at me!"

When asked to back, the pony should first be asked to step forward if he is stretched, then backed. He should back up easily, willingly, and steadily—he should not throw up his head and rush backward, nor back erratically. He should return to line and set up as before immediately after completing his back up.

Equipment

As would be expected in a gig class, the pony should wear a gig harness. This consists of his usual bridle, but with a gig bit, which is a slight variation of the liverpool. A Buxton bit may also be used but is not considered quite as proper as the gig bit. Blinkers in a gig class are usually of square pattern, but may be round or hatchet shaped. A plain bridoon is called for.

The collar should be of Kay type, black patent leather and must be a good fit for the pony. Brass hames will normally be used with this harness and should fit well into the groove of the collar. A kidney chain with a kidney-link ring connects the hames at the bottom of the collar. A long standing martingale running from the bellyband through the kidney ring attached by a loop to the bottom of the noseband. The traces should be of good sturdy quality, capable of pulling the gig used with a safety margin.

The backpad should be heavier than usual. A straight pad of at least four inches in width will quite often have sliding shaft loops. These loops can be french, tilbury or open style and are usually much heavier than normal. They are held down by a second bellyband.

The crupper strap is slightly heavier than that used in light vehicles and the crupper is the stand up type of spoon crupper. A kicking strap is always worn in gig harness and is fitted on the crupper strap a few inches in front of the forks, then down to the shafts where it is secured firmly. The kicking strap should be of a width and strength capable of restraining the horse should he actually kick.

There are several types of gig, but the most popular and best known is the Stanhope. Gigs have different shafts than ordinary carts. The front ends of the shafts are bent downward, accentuating the steeper than usual upward bend just back of the shaft stops. This distinctive bend provides security for the shaft loops because it decreases the danger of their sliding off if a trace breaks. It also provides a safe vehicle for a tandem hitch.

Usually carried in a gig, but not absolutely a requirement, are a small kit of tools and a clock on the dash.

If a groom is included in the turnout (some shows specify a groom—who rides in the gig with driver—while others do not) he should be in full dress livery. Full livery consists of a close fitting body coat with buttons to match the hardware on the harness, white breeches, black boots with tan tops, white stock, black silk top hat, and brown leather gloves. He sits on the left side of the gig with arms folded across his chest. In the lineup he dismounts and stands at the pony's head.

Pair of Hackney Ponies (maiden, novice limit)

This class consists of two Hackney ponies shown in double harness side by side (abreast) and is sometimes called a team of Hackney ponies. The gait called for in a pair class is a park pace.

In pair classes, a difference of one-half inch is allowed in height and the taller pony should be shown on the off side. (Canadian regulations allow a difference of one inch in height.)

Pairs should exhibit the same brilliant animation and way of going as the single Hackney pony, and must work as a pair, i.e., together. Because their size (and probably type) is well matched, their stride and action will be similar. This evenness and synchronization makes the pair class a very striking and colorful one. The pair class is one in which matched white stockings on ponies really adds to the effect. With front legs lifting airily and in perfect rythmn, the similarity leads one to think of a double image or some fairyland scene.

The requirements for this class have already been discussed, as have the judging classifications—except for the added category of similarity. This refers to the "matching" of the two ponies. They should be of the same color, size, type, and should have a way of going that is very similar. The foregoing desirable points are not absolutely essential to enter the class, but they add greatly to the judge's opinion of the turnout and will undoubtedly place over a poorly matched pair.

Equipment

The harness used in a pair class is different from single harness in many respects. The two styles which are acceptable, collar and hames style, are considered more useful than the breast/collar style. They are also the age old accepted form.

For the show ring, the harness should be black with brass hardware.

The bridles used can be the same as those used for single harness, but the nosebands should buckle to the outside on each side. Buxton bits are usually worn by a pair, but Liverpool bits or other elbow style bits may be used. The buxton has a bar across the bottom which prevents the horse from getting the cheeks caught in the pole chains or pole head, which could certainly cause a serious accident.

The collar and hames are usually very fancy on a Hackney pony pair. The collars are of Kay pattern and trimmed in patent leather while the hames are made of steel and brass plated. The hames must be a good fit in the groove of the collar and are usually of kidney link style. The hames are joined at the top by a hame strap, which on double harness is put on so that it can be tightened from the outside of each horse. Hame straps must be checked regularly and kept in good condition because upon this small strap depends the safety of the turnout to a large extent.

When stopping, the pole straps or chains pull forward on the hames via the kidney link at the bottom, which in turn pulls on the hame strap at the top. The traces are fastened to the hames on the draft ring (located about a third of the way up from the bottom of the hames), and are usually fastened by a trace clip which is riveted to the trace. Double traces are often of two separate pieces: the front part joining the hames called the hame tug, and into which the trace itself buckles. The buckle on the hames tug is back far enough to be in line with the backpad and has a "D" on top and bottom of the long buckle. The top part of the "D" buckles to the tug strap on the backpad and the lower part has the bellyband sewn or buckled to it. The trace is buckled onto the hame tug and is adjustable at this point. The trace ends can be of two types: either the slotted style for use with a singletree or the english style with square metal "D" through which the trace end is passed and which fits around a roller bolt fixed on the splinter bar of the buggy. If hitched to a show buggy the traces need not be of any heavier weight than the usual style for single harness.

The breastplate or false martingale is always used with pair harness. This strap goes from the bellyband up to and around the bottom of the collar and often has a fancy patent leather drop hanging down about 4 inches. This breastplate keeps the collar in place, otherwise it could slide up the horse's neck when stopping. It should be adjusted just tight enough to allow a handwidth between it and the horse's chest.

The backpad on double harness is usually very lightweight and narrow as it has very little to do except hold the traces more or less in place and provide terrets for the reins to pass through. The backpad is usually trimmed in patent leather and has ordinary crupper strap and crupper attached.

The reins used with double harness are different from single harness—there is no inside rein as such on a pair. The outside rein is an ordinary rein put on in the usual manner except that with collar and hames, the rein passes through the top ring on the hames before buckling onto the bit. The outside rein is called the draft rein. Coupling reins (short reins that connect the two horses together so that they can be steered as one) buckle onto his outside rein. The outside rein, the draft rein, has several holes in it starting about half way back which allow for adjustment of the coupling reins. The coupling reins should be run from the bit through the ring on the opposite horse's hames, then through the inside rein terret on the opposite horse, and then to the draft rein.

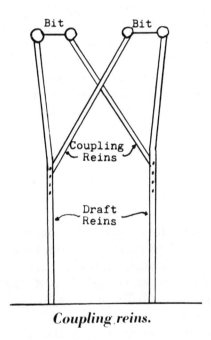

Coupling reins.

Great care must be taken to get the right length for these coupling reins to achieve proper control. Some experimenting will have to be done before the proper hole for adjustment can be determined. If one pony is bigger than the other coupling reins will not be put on in the same holes on each draft rein. Similarly if one horse carries his head much higher it will have to be taken into account. Some people like to have their pony's head bent very slightly inwards. This is done by clever use of the couplers. However, you must be careful about this as it can become a habit with the pony and one that is definitely *not* desired when driving him in single harness. I prefer to see a pair driven straight ahead with no inward pull at their heads.

The ponies are connected to the pole either by pole chains or a neck yoke and pole straps. Whichever method is used, the length of the pole strap is important. It must be adjusted so that the vehicle cannot run up onto the heels of the animals, but should not be tight enough to always be pulling forward and upwards on the pony's collar. If pole chains are used in conjunction with a steel pole head, make sure the hook faces downward, otherwise the ponies could catch their bits in it.

Breeching is not worn in pony pairs.

Pairs are shown to a Viceroy show buggy, the same buggy as described for single harness ponies, except that it is fitted with doubletrees and two singletrees or splinter bar with roller bolts. These doubletrees are connected to the rear of the pole. The pole for a Viceroy should be the lightweight variety. Either style is correct and one works as well as the other. Personal preference decides which one will be used, or perhaps more realistically one might have to take whichever was readily available.

Pair of Hackney ponies, (Ladies or Amateur)

This class is shown to a Viceroy show buggy or other appropriate vehicle. It is not an appointment class. The ponies are required to show all around action at a park pace and not faster. Ponies are required to be driven in the half cheek position with side checks and appear to have perfect mouths. They must stand quietly and back easily. They are judged on manners—the qualification of paramount importance—quality, and performance.

In this class the ponies must stand checked up while in the lineup. One attendant may stand the ponies on their feet and thereafter must remain at least two paces distant from the heads.

Stallions are prohibited in Ladies classes.

Pair of Hackney Ponies (open)

In this class the ponies are shown to a suitable four-wheeled vehicle

Pair of Hackney Ponies. "Cambridge Wally's Pride," and "Appollo's Spring Cheer." All-American Pair for 1976. Owned and driven by William A. Harris, Erin, Ontario.

with side checks. They are judged on performance, quality, similarity, and manners.

Tandem Hackney Ponies

In a tandem class, two ponies are shown one in front of the other. Tandem consists of two entries and should not be confused with the random class which implies three shown one in front of the other. The tandem class is a pretty class to watch and a most difficult class to drive. It requires great driving skill and well-trained ponies.

The driver does not have great control over the lead pony, who must be a very well reined and biddable animal. The leader of the pair ought also to be a bit smaller than the wheeler and possess a great deal of brilliance and animation. The wheeler usually has a bit more substance and is slightly larger than the leader. He must also be of proper size for the shafts and have the power to both control the vehicle and perform the work in hand. He ought to have good action, form, and style as well. A smart leader is absolutely essential for a good tandem turnout. The ponies do not have to be the same color, but uniformity adds greatly to the overall picture and is considered in the judging.

Tandem Hackneys are shown to a suitable two-wheeled vehicle with side checks. They are shown at a smart trot and are judged on performance, quality, uniformity, and manners.

Equipment

The harness used on a tandem pair can be of two types. Both ponies can wear collar and hames style or the leader can wear breast collar while the wheeler wears collar and hames. Either way is correct as long as the rest of the harness is matched to the style.

We will discuss first of all the type where both wear collar and hames. The bridle on the leader will be a normal Hackney bridle, such as those worn in the other classes described, used with a Buxton bit. The collar and hames is the same as that used in pair classes. The traces on the leader will be much longer since they have to reach back onto the wheelers hame tug in order to leave some room between the ponies. The leader will also have retaining straps to hold the traces in place to prevent getting a leg over while turning. One strap, a hip strap with trace carriers, runs over his croup and supports the traces just behind the loin area. Another strap runs from about the middle of each trace down to the center of the bellyband to keep the traces from sliding up over the pony's back if he turns too sharply or acts up in any way. The reins on the lead pony are very long because they must reach back to the driver's hands. The backpad on the leader is usually of single harness width, i.e., slightly wider than team harness to more evenly match the wheeler's pad. The trace loops are usually from six to eight inches long and ought to have enough give to permit the trace to run freely through them.

The wheeler is harnessed very similarly to the gig pony. He will wear the same bridle as the leader, with Buxton bit, but in addition his bridle will have extra rein loops or carriers slung either from the crown piece or with rings fitted to a throat latch. These rings, or drops, must be of a size large enough to permit the reins to move easily and with no restraint.

These rings are usually mounted at a height so that the reins from the leader pass about the center of the wheeler's blinkers. The collar and hames are the same as for the gig pony, the hame tug having an additional ring or dee to which the leader's trace attaches. The backpad is either a gig pad or a single harness style of slightly more width. It has the additional feature of tandem rein terrets—usually a larger ring with a bar set in right across the center. The wheeler's reins go through the bottom half and the leader's reins come back from the drops on the wheeler's bridle and through the top half of the terrets. The driver has two pair of reins in his hands, a separate set for each pony. Both ponies are checked up in the usual way and at their usual height.

It is customary to bit the leader lighter than the wheeler so that he may take good contact with the hands. It is very difficult to drive and steer a tandem team in which the leader is behind the bit and out of contact. It is even more difficult if the wheeler is a puller and the leader too light!

The leader should be the more brilliant and the faster of the two ponies, as this will not only look better but be much easier to drive. The leader must also be a pony that is keen and one that does not need much urging or the wheeler may become upset and erratic in movement due to the drivers' admonitions to the lead pony.

It is equally correct in most classes to have the lead pony wear breast collar instead of collar and hames. If this style is worn, the lead pony wears exactly the same harness as described above, but breast collar and extra long traces are substituted for the neck collar, hames, and traces. The retaining straps connected to the traces will be the same as described above. The breast collar can be the same one as is worn in single harness with the extra long traces buckled on.

Another method of coupling the two ponies together is by means of lead bars. This is a neat looking method consisting of two singletrees joined together with a swivel hook. The one singletree connects to the hame tugs of the wheeler while the leader is hitched to the front bar or singletree. This method permits the driver to use ordinary length traces instead of the extra long ones which are sometimes hard to procure these days. The only drawback of this method is that if the wheeler is a real high stepper, he may hit his knees on the bar. That is not only noisy but disconcerting to the pony. Lead bars are often seen in Europe, as it is a popular method in that country.

The vehicle used for a tandem pair is sometimes a gig, a high dog cart, or the old-fashioned type of tandem cart. It is usually a two-wheeler for this class, but a four-wheeled vehicle is sometimes correct. If a two-wheeled cart is used, the higher the better (up to a point) because it is easier to drive from a higher vantage point in this type of reinsmanship.

It is usual to wear a breastplate on the lead pony with breast collar style of harness. It helps keep the harness in place and adds a balance to the turnout because the wheeler also wears one with his collar. On most breast collars there is a small dee on the lower edge to which the martingale attaches.

The whip carried by the driver of a tandem team is somewhat different than the single Hackney whip. It has a much longer lash, one that is long enough to reach the leader. The use of this type of whip is an art in itself and one that is described in great detail in "Hints on Driving" by Captain C. Morley Knight (Reference 1).

Training

Considerable training is necessary before the two ponies will be able to move off smoothly as one. This is something that only practice and more practice can perfect. The leader must not be allowed to rush off first or else he will pull on the wheeler (causing much grief in that direction); nor must the wheeler be allowed to rush up into the lead pony before he gets moving. It stands to reason that both ponies must be extremely well trained in single harness before they can work really well as a tandem. Work in double harness is also excellent training for the propective tandem team. The driver, too, has a great deal of practicing to do before he becomes proficient at the job since a tandem is one of the most difficult of turnouts to drive.

Make sure you have a helper when you attempt to hitch tandem. It is impossible to hitch the two alone and get safely into the cart and assemble reins, whip and all, by oneself. Hitch the wheeler first and bring his reins back into the cart. Have your helper hold the leader in position while you hitch him properly and run his reins back to the cart, via the drops on the wheeler's bridle and through the tandem terrets of his pad. Have the helper stand at the leader's head until you are safely in position in the cart and have your two sets of reins properly positioned and under control. When ready to move off, have the helper lead the lead pony off the first few steps so as to assure a smooth start. Practice starts and stops with the helper at hand to assist for several times until the ponies learn how to manage these commands in unison and without jerkiness or becoming upset. Once in motion the tandem only needs practice on the drivers part to become adept and smooth. Turns should be practiced until the driver can manage this movement without danger of the leader getting over the traces or the wheeler running up into the leader half way around the turn.

Depending on the vehicle used, the groom should be either full dress livery (as described for the gig class) or stable livery. Some examples of stable livery are a dark suit, white shirt, dark tie, brown leather gloves, bowler hat; or a brown jacket, jodhpur breeches or drill trousers, white shirt, tie or stock, brown leather gloves, and bowler hat. Other styles of conservative stable dress are also acceptable. A Park Tandem would call for full dress livery, whereas a Road Tandem could use either, and a Sporting Tandem calls for a Stable Livery.

Collection of Three Hackney Ponies

As the title implies, this class consists of three Hackney ponies, shown

Tandem of Hackney Ponies. "Cambridge Wally's Pride," leader, and "Appollo's Spring Cheer," wheeler. All American Tandem for 1976, owned by William A. Harris, Erin, Ontario and driven by Mr. Matt McDougall.

either as three singles or as a pair and a single. It is judged on performance of the ponies as a unit, ability to maintain proper distance between ponies, uniformity, and quality. Each exhibitor is required to give a solo performance of his ponies as a unit both ways of the ring.

The ponies are shown, harnessed, and driven the same as described earlier in single Hackney pony and pair Hackney ponies. The fact that they are judged on uniformity means that the drivers will have to have had some experience working together to be able to keep the ponies going as a unit. They must be able to keep the same distance between the ponies during all the maneuvres asked for by the judge or those decided upon for the solo performance.

Hackney Ponies are also shown in Four-in-Hands, in a Park Drag or a Road Coach. These classes are beyond the scope of this text, but the reader who wishes to show his ponies in this exciting and very lovely class would do well to read the chapters on same in "On the Box Seat" by the well known authority Mr. Tom Ryder. (Reference 2).

6
THE HARNESS PONY

A Harness Pony may be any breed or combination of breeds of pony. Usually Hackney blood is predominate in order to produce the high and snappy action demanded by this class. Combinations with Welsh or Shetland are the usual mixes used to achieve the harness ponies shown today. The harness pony is expected to show the same high and lofty action of the Hackney pony—animation, presence, and brilliance. Although they are a smaller edition of the Hackney pony, their way of going is the same and powerful hock action is again a crucial factor in obtaining the necessary impulsion for the front end to show its magnificence.

The maximum height allowed for a harness pony is 12:2 hands. Quite often one sees little fellows of around 11:3 or 12 hands—exquisite and delicate looking miniatures who are very finely made all over. Their tremendous conformation and way of going belies their size; they surely think they are eight feet tall!

Harness ponies are shown with full manes and tails—the rule books says "long mane and undocked tail." A pony is not permitted to show in both the Harness pony section and the Hackney pony section. Harness ponies usually are shown with colored ribbon braided into their forelock and hanging down about 8–10 inches. This is tucked through the browband and out the same side as that on which the mane falls. One braid is also braided into the very front bit of their mane, usually of two or three colored ribbon braided flat and with snipped ends. The effect, as these little fellows strut around the ring, is one of great color and style.

The tails of the Harness Ponies are left long and encouraged to grow abundantly. They are shown in a high tail crupper and often wear a false tail laced on over the real one to produce the added length or thickness desired. It seems to be desirable at present at least, to have the pony's tail reach to the ground if not longer. When in motion it presents a very pleasing and flowing look. The tails are kept braided with cloth interbraided for support when not showing in order to save the hair, as this is one of the Harness Pony's crowning assets. For extra protection, special tail bags are marketed, in which the tail is placed and the bag tied shut at the top. Needless to say, the ponies are not turned out this way, but are kept in stalls. Show ponies are seldom ever turned out because all energy should be saved for the show ring and not wasted running around a pasture or paddock. Their daily workouts are considered to be enough exercise for them.

The tails must be gradually accustomed to being put in the high tail crupper. Usually this is done by wearing a tail set for some time previously. If the pony has been nicked the tail will be more flexible and easily held in this position. A real kicking spree can result from putting a pony's tail in a high crupper with no preliminary initiation!

Harness ponies are shown in the same classifications as Hackney Ponies, *except* there is no Gig class or Collection of Ponies for the Harness Pony division. All the classes discussed in the previous chapter have their counterpart in Harness Ponies except for these two.

Equipment

The harness used for Harness Ponies is the same as for Hackney Ponies. It is scaled down slightly because of their smaller size, but otherwise the same specifications hold.

The show buggy used is also the same, a Viceroy, which as a rule is a scaled down version. The Viceroy used with Harness Ponies often has 20 or 24 inch wheels rather than the usual 26 inch size.

The judging of Harness ponies is determined by the same qualifications as those for Hackneys and in the same order of importance. The same rule applies to the showing of Harness Ponies by ladies, juniors and amateurs—they are not allowed to show a stallion.

Training

It follows that if the classes are the same and the harness ponies are predominantly Hackney, the training is along the same lines as that for the Hackney. Harness ponies are driven the same way as Hackney Ponies. The driver strives to get the most animation, brilliance, presence, and action, and as in the Hackney pony classes, speed is neither desirable nor requested. Park pace and "show your pony" are the two gaits called for and no faster gait should be performed.

Harness pony to a Viceroy. "Appollo's Heir," Winning Harness Pony Champion 1972. Owned by Mrs. W. P. Roth, San Mateo, Calif., and driven by Mr. Stan Morrison.

7
THE STANDARDBRED HORSE

The first Standardbred Stud Book was formed in 1871. Decades before that date this unique breed was making a considerable impression upon the young nation that nurtured it. The trotting horse played a large part in the history of the country both socially and economically.

The breed evolved from a purely Thoroughbred horse who never raced on the trot—the immortal Messenger—a blue blooded member of the English Stud Book and the great grandsire of a horse named Hambletonian. From four distinguished sons of Hambletonian, all present day trotting and pacing Standardbreds derive. The name Standardbred comes from the fact that sire and dam were mated to produce a horse capable of trotting or pacing a mile within the prescribed limits of a certain standard of time. The original standard was adopted by the National Association of Trotting Horse Breeders in 1879, establishing a record of 2:30 for the mile distance as a base. This appeared in Volume 4 of *The Trotting Register,* and in this volume Hambletonian was assigned number 10, a number to become so very famous in later years. Hambletonian's sire was Abdallah, number 1.

Arabian blood played a large part in the Standardbred breed, as it did in so many other breeds. The Darley Arabian founded the line that led to Messenger, and thence to Hambletonian. The connecting link was the Darley Arabian's brilliant son, the undefeated Flying Childers, one of the great race horses of all time and still a legend on the British turf.

The Morgans also helped establish the Standardbred breed. They provided a trotting gait that is typified now by the round, slashing front action of the modern trotter who has the extension of the Messengers as well as the more rounded action of the Morgans.

Hambletonian was never raced and was not a handsome horse. He had a very plain head and there was nothing refined about his conformation. He reeked of brute power with massive quarters, strong bone, and heavily muscled forearms which set off the trotting pitch he and so many of his descendants possessed. He stood 15:1¼ at the withers and 15:3¼ behind, a two inch slope from rump to withers!

In 1895 a horse named Peter the Great was to change the course of Harness racing history and live to establish the most prominent trotting line the sport has ever known. Except for the few that descend from George Wilkes, all prominent male line trotting blood in America descends from Peter the Great.

The pacer has become very popular in modern harness racing. In fact it is not uncommon to see eight of nine races on a parimutuel track card devoted to pacers. Fitted with hobbles that enable them to maintain gait in tight situations that would send a trotter into a flying break, the pacer is the darling of the American public.

The Canadian horses, sometimes called French–Canadians, played a large part in establishing the pacer within the Standardbred breed. The original Tom Hal, founder of the Hal family, was identified as a Canadian horse. A generation later, one of his offspring sired the brothers Little Brown Jug (2:11¾) and Brown Hal (2:12). Little Brown Jug, a gelding, was the first world champion of the Hal line. The only other Canadian horse that left a lasting imprint on the modern Standardbred was a black horse known as Old Pilot and who resembled in type and conformation the French–Canadian pacer. In 1832 he is said to have paced a mile in 2:26 hitched to a wagon. He could also trot. This horse was the forerunner of Peter the Great—his grandsire!

Almost sixty years ago Dan Patch went a mile in 1:55¼ and we have chipped less than two seconds from that record! The world record for trotters was held by Greyhound (1:55¼) until a couple of years ago.

The Standardbred horse is not always beautiful, but he was not evolved in that direction. His breeding and improvement has always been for speed and more speed. Beauty and elegance do not help very much in the speed line, and the Standardbred is first and foremost a race horse. In the eyes of his owners and promoters he is considered a very handsome animal and indeed there have been many extremely good-looking Standardbreds.

The predominant color of Standardbreds is bay or brown. They usually stand from about 14:2 to 15:3 hands and weigh between 900 and 1,150 pounds. A fairly straight head is a distinctive feature of the Standardbred; he should have a good width between the eyes, wide nostrils, and medium sized ears (although long ears are not uncommon in the breed.) For racing purposes he should have a good width of chest because this will give him more clearance when travelling and he'll be less likely to hit himself.

He should be straight in the knees and have a good angle of pastern.

The angle of the pastern is very important, as is the length. The pastern is the shock absorber of the horse, and if the pastern is too straight there will not be enough spring to relieve the strain. On the other hand, if it is too long there will be too much strain exerted and tendon problems will result.

The Standardbred should have a good deep shoulder with a symmetrical slope to it. As it is the prime area of driving power in front, it should have a powerful look to it and be well muscled. A sloping shoulder indicates a bolder and longer stroke which is especially desirable in a trotter. A straighter shoulder usually means that the horse hits the ground straighter and harder and has more chance of going lame.

He should have a fairly long neck set well onto his shoulder. A deep heart girth is most desirable in a harness horse and often indicates staying power and stamina. A trotter should be long barrelled because this will help him avoid hitting his knees, but a pacer can be shorter barrelled. A good croup with a bit of slope to it is usual in a Standardbred as well as powerful muscular quarters. The legs should go straight down from the hocks and the thighs and gaskins should be well developed and muscular.

Racing

Standardbreds are divided into two categories: trotters and pacers. Trotters go with a diagonal gait while pacers travel with lateral stride. Not too long ago trotters and pacers raced together against each other, but now this practice is discontinued and each type races against itself. There are various classifications in which they race for varying amounts of "purses" or prize moneys, that are governed in part by the horse's winnings and time record. A full explanation and description of this somewhat complicated system is beyond the scope of this book but the author recommends that the reader who is interested in learning these details read the excellent publication "Care and Training of the Trotter and Pacer" (Reference 3).

There are many race tracks in the nation and Harness Racing is one of the biggest industries at present. Records are being set and broken frequently and the caliber of the harness horses is constantly being improved. With the advent of synthetic all-weather tracks and proper night lighting, races can be run at any time and most tracks feature cards nightly rather than just on weekends as used to be the case. Horses are shipped from track to track, sometimes by air, as modern transportation and shrinking distances make racing possible on two tracks thousands of miles apart on consecutive nights. Top drivers often drive on two different tracks in two completely different areas (or even countries) on the same day!

Equipment

Racing harness consists of bridle, breast collar and traces, backpad, bellyband and crupper for the basic harness. All sorts of straps and extra gear are worn by trotters and pacers, but for the moment we will describe the basic harness.

The bridle is a standard blind bridle, or open if preferred (as some trainers and drivers prefer open bridles) with overcheck, usually the five buckle style of overcheck, snaffle bit and check bit. The breast collar is very fine and narrow, about 1¼ inches wide, sewn on traces with slot adjustments on the ends. The neck strap is very fine and buckles on both sides. The backpad is fine and fairly narrow, about 2¼ inches, with open style shaft loops, crupper strap and sewn on crupper. The bellyband has wrap straps, and buckles are shielded by extensions of the bellyband that lace up outside the buckle. All straps are doubled on race harness for strength and safety. Thimbles are buckled onto the dees of the backpad. Reins are normal length with adjustable hand holds part way up, black front parts with tan hand parts usually, or sometimes all russett. A saddlecloth is worn under the backpad. This gives the horse's back protection and is usually in the driver's stable or racing colors. Patent leather is not used on racing harness nor is brass hardware. The harness is made of good quality english leather and kept very soft and pliable, and the fittings are usually nickel or chrome. Stainless steel is becoming more popular recently. Head numbers are worn during a race and clip onto the crown of the bridle. The same number is worn under the saddlecloth as well. This completes the basic harness as worn by both pacers and trotters. Some extra items worn by the breed are outlined as follows:

Trotters—elbow boots, quarter boots, shin boots, speedy cut boots, scalping boots, toe weights, and suspenders to hold up some of the types of boots worn.

Pacers—knee boots, knee boot suspenders, shin boots, ankle boots, bell boots, coronet boots, brace bandages, and of course hobbles and their hangars.

All of these various boots and pieces are not necessarily worn at the

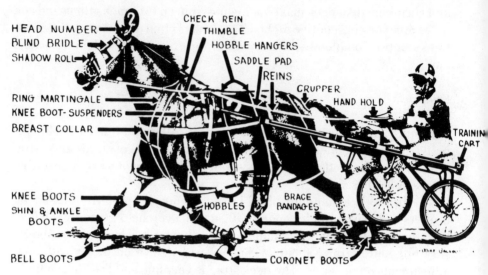

HEAD NUMBER
BLIND BRIDLE
SHADOW ROLL
RING MARTINGALE
KNEE BOOT-SUSPENDERS
BREAST COLLAR
KNEE BOOTS
SHIN & ANKLE BOOTS
BELL BOOTS
CHECK REIN
THIMBLE
HOBBLE HANGERS
SADDLE PAD
REINS
CRUPPER
HAND HOLD
TRAINING CART
HOBBLES
BRACE BANDAGES
CORONET BOOTS

EQUIPMENT COMMONLY WORN BY
THE PACER
Pacer in harness.

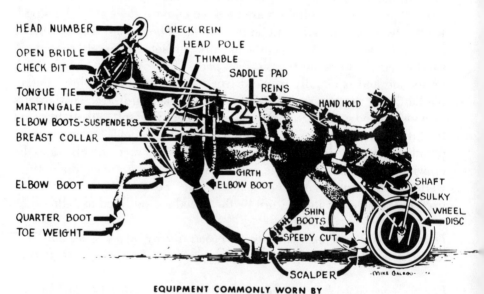

HEAD NUMBER
OPEN BRIDLE
CHECK BIT
TONGUE TIE
MARTINGALE
ELBOW BOOTS-SUSPENDERS
BREAST COLLAR
ELBOW BOOT
QUARTER BOOT
TOE WEIGHT
CHECK REIN
HEAD POLE
THIMBLE
SADDLE PAD
REINS
HAND HOLD
GIRTH
ELBOW BOOT
SHAFT
SULKY
WHEEL DISC
SHIN BOOTS
SPEEDY CUT
SCALPER

EQUIPMENT COMMONLY WORN BY
THE TROTTER
Trotter in harness.

same time, but on occasion one does see most of these things on a race horse. All have their functions and if a horse is having problems in that area, the protective boot or piece of equipment will be put on immediately. Contrary to general talk, usually by non–harness types, these boots and other equipment do not bother or deter the Harness horse one bit. If they did, it stands to reason in an industry where speed is the main factor anything that would cause loss of it or damage to a horse would not be used. All of these rather intricate looking pieces of equipment have been designed by people associated with the sport and are made for specific purposes.

Training

Once broken to harness, the Standardbred undergoes a rigorous training schedule. He is jogged six days a week and turned and trained usually once each time in the early stages. Once he is used to his shoes his trainer has to find out if and where the colt is going to hit himself when training or racing.

To protect the colt, usually shin boots of one sort or another are worn on trotters and scalping boots behind. If he is going to his knees, knee boots will be worn either on one leg or both. Many pacers wear quarter boots in front because of the danger of cross firing. A variety of boots—passing boots, shin boots with speedy cut attachments with half hock or full hock protection, ankle boots, high scalpers—all are used for the specific protection of one part or another of the horse's legs. Whatever boot is used has to be properly fitted and the horse accustomed to its use.

Shoeing has to be precise to the fraction of the ounce as does the length of toe. If you take as little as an eighth of an inch too much off the front toe of a trotting colt you can change his gait entirely and get him completely out of kilter. The same thing can happen in a pacer by leaving the toe an eighth of an inch too long. Trainers usually keep a card on every horse in their barn specifying the length of toe all around, the weight of shoe, type of shoe, and any remarks. After each shoeing the card is brought up to date and all details entered. In this way there is little margin for error, and much better results can be obtained on the track than by the old hit and miss method. A horse's foot must be kept in good condition. Most trainers use a mixture of clay to pack the foot after each daily workout.

There is always controversy about blind bridles versus open bridles. Whichever works best on your colt is naturally the one that should be used. With a nervous colt, you are probably better off training him in an open bridle so that he can see what is coming up behind him and not be frightened by a noise he hears and cannot see. However, most colts keep their attention better if a blind bridle is used.

By now the colt is likely training a mile around 3:20. This is gradually worked down to about 2:50 as the colts are trained a mile about three times a week. The other three days are jogging days when the colts are not brushed or trained. Right about now you are trying to find out whether or not your colt will need more weight to train faster or just how he is going to develop. You are trying to establish a rythmn which is helped by shoeing, length of foot, and the boots worn. Without rythmn a colt is uncoordinated and speed cannot result.

After about a month, the colt is ready for two-mile training miles, usually done twice a week. These miles are not run all at once, but with a breather between during which the colt is put back in his stall, stripped, washed, blanketed, and let breathe. During the breather period all boots, harness and clothing worn by the colt is thoroughly cleaned. Hobbles, especially have to be carefully examined. Tight hobbles will chafe a horse, and the horse should be examined for evidence of chafing. Hobbles should be kept scrupulously clean. Talcum powder is used considerably on hobbles and on the horses' legs under the hobbles to prevent chafing.

He is let rest for about forty minutes then harnessed, taken back onto the track and trained another mile. These miles are done in about 2:50 to begin with, dropping two or three seconds a week as the colt develops muscles, manners, and ability. These double training miles are called "repeating" in harness racing language.

When the colt's training time is down to 2:35 the trainer usually starts to go three training trips instead of two. This stage goes on down until 2:25 is reached. These training trips are done as follows: the first one at 2:50, the second one at 2:40 and the third one at whatever speed to which the trainer has decided to drop the colt. He works down to 2:25 gradually, of course, taking about three weeks to arrive at that speed. Pacers will reach this speed easier than trotters as it is easier to keep them on gait. The trainer stays for about three weeks at this level of speed. He then starts to go a fast mile and a slow mile, the fast workout being in 2:25 and the slow one in about 2:28—not much difference, but very noticeable to the colt. When these miles are done, quite often the last eighth would be in 14 or 15 seconds. All this depends upon the colt, how he is taking the faster work, and how he is travelling. Some colts can be asked for more speed where others cannot. The trainer has to know his colt and decide which is best.

It is good practice to work colts with other colts or horses. They must get used to horses coming up behind and sitting on the outside as well as seeing them out in front. If they train this way it won't excite them in a real race.

After about three more weeks at the 2:25 level, the trainer will start to move his colt down towards the 2:15 mark. Again, it is done gradually and at the colt's own speed. At about 2:19 or so, the colt will be worked in four trips. This is good training for them because if they are racing in heats later on they will have to go several trips. When going four trips, they are usually done in this order: first trip 2:50, second 2:35, third (and fastest) 2:20, and the last one, the "cooling heat" around 2:25.

From now until they are ready to race (about a month) the colts are brushed a bit faster and moved out more. They are asked to leave a bit faster, away from the wire, and do the half in around 1:10 (then varying the other half, ending with about 1:05 for the second half.) This time is varied, of course. Some days the mile will be in 2:12. It all depends upon the individual colt and how he works.

Before the colt is ready to race, he must be trained to follow a starting gate. This is a most important part of his training and one that should be done as often as possible with a youngster. The procedure is done step by step so that the youngster is introduced to the gate in an easy manner and not frightened and perhaps put off for a long time because of it. While jogging the colt, have the gate driven onto the track and circle the track while the colts follow it at a safe distance. Each time the gate is brought onto the track, the colts will follow it, and after a couple of weeks they will drive right up behind it with no fear or problems. Be sure to do all this at a slow jog and not rush the colt into the gate before he has accepted it.

The next step is to introduce the colts to the gate in their training miles. At this point they would be going in about 2:35. It is a good plan to have the colts (it is better to have several colts working at one time) line up behind the gate and follow it around the track once before they start their training mile. The gate should be positioned in the same place as it would be in an actual race, which is usually at the three-quarter pole. The driver of the gate must have great tact and sensibility and not take off out of the field after he has dropped the colts. He will have taken them one and a half times around the track gradually picking up speed and moving off out of the way. If he gunned the gate and got out of there in a cloud of dust the colts would likely end up in a real fright and could hurt themselves badly (besides getting a bad idea of the gate for future racing). A colt has to be taught manners in a gate. This is accomplished in conjunction with the gate driver's assistance.

By now the colts are ready to be given the actual type of gate training such as would be used in a race. They are driven down to the gate as usual (which is in position at the three-quarter pole), stopped and allowed to look it over, then turned and driven back to the gate where they stop again to look it over. This time the gate driver starts up the gate, very slowly at first, then picks up a little speed as he goes on. At the starting line he gradually pulls away and the colts go their training mile. After a few such dry runs, the colts are fairly well broken to the gate and ought to be no trouble.

The colt should now be ready to race. Before the race he is usually warmed up in three heats, depending again upon the individual. The heats would be divided in approximately this way: the first one in 2:50, the second in 2:35, and the last in 2:25. Keep in mind that this is his first race—later on in the season his third warm up heat will go much faster than 2:25, likely around 2:15.

The race is run and our colt behaves well, is cooled out properly and put away.

One aspect of training that should perhaps be talked about a little is the cooling out of a horse after he has worked. This is a most important aspect of the training and one that can lead to problems if not properly carried out.

When the colt is through his workout, he should be either bathed or cleaned with a warm wet sponge, scraped and a cooler put on. He should be walked with either one or two coolers on (depending on the weather and how hot he is) and offered a few sips of water every few minutes until he is watered out and dry. The technique of cooling out varies from trainer to trainer, but it usually take roughly an hour. In order to be cooled out properly the horse's body must feel both dry and cool to the touch and he must refuse water.

Now let us follow the sequence of his training once he has been started in an actual race. Let's say he raced a certain night of the week, for instance Monday. On Tuesday, the next day, he was just walked for about half an hour while the rest of the time he was left to sleep, rest and let down after his effort the day before. On Wednesday, he is jogged about three miles. Thursday he is trained. (How he is trained will depend upon how he raced on the Monday night). He will be jogged about three miles on Friday and again on Saturday. Sunday is his day off. If he is to be raced again on the Monday he is usually walked about half an hour in the morning. Then the colt makes this second start and the inbetween work begins all over again. If the colt is not to be raced again for two weeks, the trainer will likely let up on him a bit in the interim. He would probably be jogged every day but trained only once a week.

The two year old is now established on the race track. His work in the future will vary with both type of race and the amount of work needed for the particular colt. He should not be raced too hard as a two year old. If his trainer chooses the horse's races carefully, as a three year old he will be sound and ready to really put in a rigorous season at the raceways.

Sometimes little problems arise in the training program, and one of the most common of these is a horse who carries his head to one side or holds it crookedly. There are several types of bits to help correct this condition, as well as bit burrs, rein burrs or pole burrs. There are also strategically placed shadowrolls, and finally the head pole. The head pole is a small pole about the size of a pool cue that is placed on the side of the horse's head and neck, running from the saddle pad up to the head halter, where it is mounted through a ring on the side. The head pole keeps a horse's head straighter by preventing him from turning his head to one side. If the horse is carrying his head to the right as most track horses will do, the head pole is placed on the left. If he holds it crooked to the left, the head pole goes on the right. The new type of modern head pole is telescopic and much handier than the older style which used to stick out in front of the horse's head and sometimes became caught in the starting gate. A head pole ball is often used in conjunction with the pole when a horse still wants to lean into the pole. It is a round ball with a hole through its center through which the pole is inserted. The ball hits the horse's neck as he leans into the pole and is supposed to deter him from turning his head out.

Harness horses are raced in sulkies, or bikes as they are often called. These are extremely light two-wheeled carts with pneumatic tires, weighing about forty pounds. (By comparison, a training cart would weigh around seventy-five pounds). Up until recently they mainly had wooden shafts, highly varnished and striped, or sometimes metal ones. Now fiberglas construction has entered even the racing industry and some bikes are of this type. Dimensions vary, but an average bike would be 50" wide, 27" high, and with shafts 87" long.

Getting a leg or foot in someone else's wheel spokes used to be a common occurrence and often caused bad accidents. This led to wheel covers or shields (a metal or synthetic round cover which bolts or snaps on to the outside of each wheel and protects the spokes and prevents a foot entering). This invention has gone a long way to make racing safer. Hard hats worn by racing drivers has also eliminated much hardship and damage. They may not look as jaunty or debonair as the old-fashioned peaked harness caps, but they certainly give a lot more protection. The driver still wears the silks or colored jacket so long associated with the sport. These colors are usually individual stable or owner colors registered in their name. Usually of bright combinations, they add dash and easy identification to the horses in a race. The saddlecloth is usually of the same color. Head numbers are worn in a race by a horse; one clips onto his bridle crown and stands upright with a number on each side, the other fastens under his saddlecloth and is quickly identifiable from a distance.

Standardbred Pacer in a sulky. "C. F. Sincous," pacer, owned, trained and driven by Mr. Gordon Cousins, Delta, British Columbia. Racing at Sacramento, Calif.

The horses usually are picked up from the three-quarter pole by the gate and the race is from the wire once around to the wire again. Often there is a photo finish where the winner is not announced until the picture is developed and examined by the stewards. Many races are won by the proverbial nose. A commentator usually gives a running narration of the race as it progresses around the track including pertinent times to various distances. As the three-quarter pole is reached and horses start moving out for the finish, the crowd literally goes wild and the noise and din are terrific.

This can be a traumatic experience for a colt's first race—but one he must get used to because it happens every time. After awhile the horses race better with lots of noise and excitement—especially in the home-stretch. The horses gradually slow down after passing the wire, and are stopped and turned in an eighth-mile or so. The winner is driven back to the stands, and escorted to the winners circle to be photographed and publicly acclaimed as the winner. All the vital statistics are given over the P.A. system at this time. After he is led back to the ready area, he is usually given one of several tests for signs of drugging or other illegal procedures that are sometimes practiced. He is then driven or led back to the barns and put up for the night.

8
THE ROADSTER

The Roadster should be a standard or non-standard bred horse, of attractive appearance, balanced in conformation, and with manners which make him a safe risk in the ring. He should travel easily and at speed. Usually between fifteen and sixteen hands and weighing 800 to 1,200 pounds, Roadsters wear long tails and natural manes.

The action of a roadster should be free, easy, straight, well-balanced, and not excessively high. Animation, brilliance and presence should be characteristic of his gait, and he should have good manners. Conformation-wise, the Roadster ought to have a well-chiseled head, alert ears, a fine throat area, and display a fine and fairly long neck. He ought to have a deep chest, sloping shoulder, and well-defined withers. His ability to move out well and freely will stem from this area. He should have a short back, well proportioned, strong hind quarters, and good flat bone in his legs.

Roadsters are shown either to a bike or to a road wagon. Usually the type of Roadster shown to a road wagon will be taller and have more scale.

Roadsters are shown in several classes, each class being judged on qualifications which differ in order of importance. In all classes, the gaits called for are jog trot, road gait, then at speed. The walk is seldom asked for these days, but a good walk is desirable in a Roadster. The jog trot is a medium speed gait, ground-covering, but not fast. It should be displayed with animation, brilliance and freedom of movement. It should be collected with the horse's head set and obvious power and impulsion emanating from the hind quarters. At the road gait, the speed is increased considerably and the horse must display form with great animation, good balance, and the ability to work in the turns. Roadsters should go well into the corners without side reining or breaking their gait and come out very fast in good form and with true action.

Their manners and mouths should be such that they can be taken up in the straights or at any time without severe bitting or obvious force. The stride of the Roadster should be ground-covering and easy; it must not look like an effort. His cadence should be true and even and he should move with powerful diagonals. His action should be fairly high in front—not like a Hackney by any means, but pleasingly airy and lifted—and he should work well off his hind end. The Roadster should be shown on the rail at all times except when passing. When asked to "drive on", the horse should show good speed and go in form. He must not be sprawly-gaited in front nor strung out behind, nor should he go too wide behind. Rather he should display balance, coordination, and tremendous ability. Any tendency to pace or rack on the turns, or to break or even mix the gaits will be severly penalized in a Roadster class. Their trot must be true all the time. The Roadster must stand in line quietly and back readily when asked. Headers or attendants are not allowed, and drivers must remain in their carts with the horses' heads checked up (except for a work out when the horses left in the middle may be unchecked).

The classes and specifications for roadsters are as follows:

Single Roadster is to be shown by an amateur. To be shown to bike (or wagon) at a jog trot, road gait and then at speed. The class is judged on manners, performance, speed, and quality in that order of importance.

Single Roadster appointments. This class is to be shown to a road wagon at a jog trot, road gait, and then at speed. It is judged on performance, speed, quality, manners, and appointments. (Appointments are discussed later on in this chapter).

Pairs of Roadster appointments. To be shown to a road wagon at a jog trot, road gait and then at speed. The class is judged on performance, speed, quality, manners, style, and appointments.

Single Roadster open. To be shown to bike (or wagon) at a jog trot, road gait and then at speed. It is judged on performance, speed, quality, and manners.

Equipment

The harness used on roadsters is usually a very fine, light harness. Starting with the bridle, we have box loop cheeks, patent leather blinkers of square pattern, and a Kimbal Jackson type of checkrein. A snaffle bit, either straight or jointed is used. The little check bit is a straight type, although sometimes the check is used in conjunction with a chin strap instead of a bit. A noseband or separate caveson is worn, the front of which is often made of patent leather. The breast collar has straight flaps, while traces are sometimes made round back to the flat ends. Traces may be beaded and made finely as an alternative. A full martingale is worn and all buckles should be leather or rubber-covered except the rein terrets and checkrein hook. Thimbles are worn in bike classes. The backpad is fine, usually with considerable patent leather, open shaft loops, bellyband with wrap straps, and made of fine leather. The crupper is sewn on to the crupper strap.

Reins can be of tan leather made round to the hand pieces, or of fine black beaded leather back to the hand pieces (which are tan). The buckle ends of the reins should have steel reinforcement where they buckle around the ring of the bit. All hardware should be solid brass. Breeching is not worn in bike classes, but it is a requirement in appointment classes and should be finely made and in keeping with the style and pattern of the rest of the harness. Breeching straps should always be buckled to the shafts, not snapped on as work harness.

In an appointment class several items are to be carried in the wagon. A dashboard clock should be mounted on the inside of the dash, and a kit containing hoof pick, wheel wrench, blanket pins, wire pliers, horseshoe nails, goggles, hammer, whisk, nail pliers, rasp, leather punch and sweat scraper should be fitted inside the back of the wagon. As well, there should be a road blanket, lap robe, waterproof cover, tie strap, extra horse shoes, bandages, brush, halter, and rub rags placed in convenient storage if not worn. An overcoat and hat of dark color should be worn by the driver or carried in the wagon.

In Roadster classes, quarter boots are almost always worn. These must not be weighted and should be of the standard hinged design. Boots enhance the horses' front action considerably and also give some protection in case of interference. Used in conjunction with good shoeing, boots will make the horse either reach further and lengthen his stride or develop higher action, whichever the trainer considers necessary for the horses' improvement. Usually white quarter boots are worn, because the color lends emphasis to the action and speed of the horse while in the ring. The white feet flashing at speed somehow gives the impression of a faster and more exciting gait.

In classes calling for a bike, the vehicle used is a racing sulky, often called a bike. It is a very light (about 50 pounds) two-wheeled cart to which the horse is hitched close while the driver's feet are placed in stirrups on either side of the cart. The small seat is mounted directly over the crossbar joining the forks of the wheels so that the horse's hind feet extend underneath the seat as he trots at speed. The driver's hands are seldom more than ten or twelve inches away from the horses' flanks as he holds the reins. In bike classes, the driver wears stable colors with cap and matching jacket.

In classes calling for a road wagon, or a buggy of Caffrey style, a four-wheeled vehicle is used. The road wagon is a very fancy show buggy with wooden spoked wheels instead of wire wheels as in the Fine Harness Buggy described in an earlier chapter. These wheels are of the twelve spoke variety and usually 28″ diameter. The axles and undercarriage are the same as in fine harness buggies, and the box itself is the same size. The seat of the road wagon differs in that instead of a chrome spindle-type railing, a solid, shaped, wooden, seat back and sides are made. This buggy also has a top which is always used in the down position. (The top is folded neatly over the supports.) When showing in a class calling for a road wagon, the driver would wear a business suit and a hat of his choice.

Training

Where a Roadster's training is begun will depend upon his early career, and what type of training he has already received. If he is from the track and has been trained as a harness race horse on the trot, we can easily pick up his training and channel it into the show ring. He will need considerable work in the ring at a slow and regular speed to achieve his balance on the relatively small turns. His training up until this point has been entirely for speed and he has had no experience with the sharp corners of our show rings or the necessity to work in form all the time. We will also wish to set his head in a slightly different manner and begin the process of achieving some animation. He must also be convinced that his utmost speed is no longer required or desired. If, on the other hand, our Roadster prospect has been started in the usual manner of a single driving horse and trained in a ring from the beginning, his advanced training will proceed easily and with no preconceived track habits. He should already be well along the way in the balance department and have a fairly good idea of variation of speed and response.

Whichever background our roadster has had, his training from now on will be with a show ring career in mind. The harness race horse may take longer to obtain good balance on the turns and work at show ring speeds, but he already has a great deal of knowledge that the novice horse started in the ring has yet to learn. So the training will likely take the same lines and length of time in either case.

The initial training will be jogging both ways of the ring, asking for good form and much animation, collection, and brilliance. None of this will happen overnight, but nevertheless we are asking for it and working with this aim in mind. Little by little we will achieve the amount we need.

We send the horse on in the straights and take him up in the turns enough at first to help him balance, making sure that he doesn't turn his head to the outside and side rein. If he insists on side reining, we circle him in fairly small circles about 15 or 20' in diameter, or even smaller if he still will not bend into his circle. At slow speed these circles will help him attain balance on the turns. Until he can make the turns with proper balance at a jog trot there is absolutely no use in asking him to do it at the faster speeds. That would undo all our previous training by asking for too much too soon.

Balance is an extremely important basic necessity both from the horse's point of view and the trainers. If a horse cannot balance in his turns, he will scramble, side rein, and often go down with drastic results if it happens in a big class. Consequently we must work on balance first and foremost before asking for speed.

We can initiate animation and brilliance on the straights by sending him on and taking back on the reins slightly, but we must give him strong support on his turns even after he has become a well-balanced and seasoned horse. Figure eights are a good idea for the young horse who tends to stick his head to the outside as he jogs around the ring. Using the whole ring while going down the diagonal each end will tend to straighten the horse up as the turns will change direction with each diagonal. These large figure eights help the horse to establish his gait in the turns and work off his quarters as he does it. However, he must learn to shift his weight back on the turns to take the weight off his forehand or else he will have a tendency to break in corners. His head must also be of a proper height to help him in this respect.

Vary the length of his checkrein until optimum performance results, but do it gradually (one hole at a time). If he has come from the track, the checkrein may have to be let down a fair amount to achieve the desired result. The horse should be able to flex his head and neck and bend at the poll. He should trot with his chin set and legs underneath him (which is impossible if he is checked up too high and his neck ewed from it). Some work in a bitting rig may be of considerably help in achieving a proper head set.

A great deal of jogging is necessary with short bursts of speed in the straights, while trying to maintain animation and cadence with the increased speed. Once the horse can trot his corners at a jog with balance and form, more speed can be requested. Speed should be built up gradually and include smooth transitions. Quarter boots should be worn both for protection and to produce better action. These boots must fit the horse properly. If they are too large they will not stay in place when buckled on, and if too small they will not have enough hinging movement to produce the kind of action required. They must be kept scrupulously clean because any grit inside them will act just like sandpaper on the horse's pastern area and could soon cause problems.

Now that we are working at the road gait, we should be able to make complete rounds of the ring without diminishing speed in the turns. However, this does not mean that you no longer have to support the horse in his corners—the very opposite is necessary. The horse needs even more support at speed to maintain balance and gait in the turns. He must now be encouraged to come out of his turns increasingly faster without losing cadence or form. Send him down the straights and into the turn while supporting him strongly. Then take hold and shoot him out of the other side of the turn, gradually easing up on your rein pressure as he steadies in the straight. Since this is something new, at first he will likely scramble somewhat and appear awkward coming out of the turn. But soon he will be capable of easily turning it on as long as he receives the support he needs.

You will now have to be careful not to ask for more speed in the turns every time. If this happens, the horse will begin to anticipate such and become erratic and jumpy while expecting to be asked to go on.

Once the horse becomes adept at cornering and is responsive to requests for speed, do not ask for the burst of speed coming out of the turns for awhile. Concentrate instead on other aspects of his training, such as standing quietly in the lineup. This he must do without fidgeting or being unchecked. His manners must be such that he can come directly off the rail after an exciting workout and stand quietly in the lineup without any fuss or tenseness. This he must first learn at home. Under actual show conditions in the ring, the crowd will be extremely noisy during the roadster class, as it is one of the most exciting and crowd-pleasing events at any show. The horse will have to become accustomed to this noise and stand quietly despite it. It would be of great benefit if these noisy conditions could be simulated at home in your own ring because then it will not be such a surprise and shock to the horse when he first experiences it in a show ring. Having people clap and cheer when you line up in the middle of your ring is a good way to begin, then increase it with other noises such as popping blown-up paper bags and rattling plastic bags or tin cans. Many a class is lost because a horse broke under pressure or noise in the ring, and the more we can accustom our horse to at home the safer we will be in the show ring. The noise and excitement also stimulate the horse to greater action and performance (which is a desirable thing), but before this becomes useful, the horse must not be actually fearful of the disturbance.

Returning to our horse working on the rail at road gait during our training sessions, we continue at this speed, varying it with the jog trot, until the horse can maintain this gait round after round in good form and with complete control of the corners. Now we are ready to "drive on": the most thrilling part of the Roadster class and indeed of any class in a show. Horses soon come to associate words with the action taken, and as soon as they hear the P. A. system announce these magic words, they seem to turn into veritable speed demons!

When given the word they appear to leap from the road gait into speed (and the transition must not sacrifice form). Their legs now appear to be working like pistons with regularity, rhythm, and ever-increasing spectacular speed. Now we must be "one with our horse", as he will depend greatly on his driver for support and guidance—especially in the corners. Here again there must be no side reining since the corners are where this bad habit shows up most often. And again, side reining usually stems from the same cause: asking for too much speed too soon before balance is learned and established. He must not show any tendency to rack or pace either. This, too, is a fault that often comes when a lot of speed is uncontrolled by either horse or driver.

To keep his balance and footing on the sharp corners at such speed, the horse may resort to a lateral gait, mixing his gaits as he comes out of the turn until the trot is established once more. This is a fault that will be severely penalized—and justly so—as it is an impure gait. The horse *must* trot; that is what the whole class is about.

As we ask our horse for more speed out of the road gait, we do it on the straights initially, taking back in the corners to a speed we know he can control. Gradually we let him go further into his corners before taking him back. As his control sharpens and he bends properly, more speed can be attempted in the turns. However, always take back at the first signs of trouble, otherwise your training can be set back for weeks. Once your horse develops bad habits on corners it is a difficult thing to correct. The horse gets into the habit of falling in with his quarters and leading with his inside shoulder rather than having his whole body follow the turn in an arc. The proper way is to have his head turned slightly into the turn in the direction of the turn.

Although Roadsters are only required to go at speed in one direction, I believe they should be trained and worked both ways of the ring at home. This helps keep them straight and develops more balance. In a horse show, Roadsters enter the ring clockwise and do their jog trot and road gait. They are then turned and shown at both road gait and speed in a clockwise direction.

If it is a large class, only eight horses will be asked to "drive on" at once. The remainder will line up in the center of the ring while this is going on. When lined up in a workout like this, the horses in the center are permitted to be unchecked and held at the head by their drivers. This is the only time a driver is allowed to leave his seat or uncheck his horse (except for breakage or adjustment of equipment). While horses on the rail are working out, those in the center should be well-mannered and stand quietly. This too should be practiced at home.

It is a great advantage to have several horses working with you. In this way they become accustomed to other animals working at speed in the ring at the same time. Some passing should also be practiced because quite often the first time this happens a horse will break as another one goes by. In the excitement of trotting in company at great speed, the sight of another horse going by and passing will often incite competition in the horse being passed—sometimes to the extent of breaking into a gallop. It is best to experiment at home rather than make a bad break and cause a possible pile-up in the show ring. Drivers should try to stay on the rail at all times, but especially when driving at top speed. If you absolutely have to pass the horse in front of you, care should be taken to give him a wide berth, and to make sure there is a hole for you to get back into. If left out in the center, your ring becomes so much smaller that there is no way for you to show your horse to advantage. Often too, when you pull into the center to pass the other horses space themselves out on the rail. When this happens there is no room left in which to pull back, so you are marooned out there off the rail.

During your horse's training and as you are asking for increasing animation and impulsion, careful attention should be paid to the way the horse moves behind. He should not go too wide when moving at speed. He should be going straight, and any deviation from that should be corrected—probably with shoeing. When training a young Roadster it is sometimes advisable to wear scalping boots behind to protect the foot from being hit or hurt. If a horse is consistently hitting himself behind he may begin to go wider; a habit which can quickly degenerate into an extremely wide and unsightly gait. Scalpers cannot be worn in the show ring but make good sense in training sessions.

If your Roadster is to be shown in appointment classes in a four-wheeled road wagon, it is advisable to practice at home before hand. A four-wheeled buggy is more difficult to handle than a cart so that cornering must be practiced considerably before entering the show ring. The road wagon will slide out on every corner when travelling at great speed. This requires the driver to shift his weight to the inside while he, with one foot down on the step to steady it, struggles to keep himself *in* the buggy! Since the centrifugal force is tremendous at speed, were the driver sitting unresistingly on the outside of the seat, he would likely fly right out of his buggy.

While keeping his balance at speed, the driver must not do so by hanging on his reins! This is the critical period where his horse needs the utmost support and assistance from his hands and his body position must not jeopardize this liason. By leaning into the turns and using body weight to offset the pressure on the turns, the driver can safely stay with the buggy while maintaining light and constant communication with the horse. The driver also must pay attention to just where his buggy is sliding, as he could hit another horse or buggy if passing on the corner. The action of the buggy sliding violently on the corners pulls the horse (via the shafts) in a different way from his normal everyday workouts in a cart, so he too must become familiar with the action. As the turning ability of a buggy is greatly restricted, the driver must keep this in mind before attempting any sharp turns such as those he could easily make in a two-wheeled cart. A four-wheeled show buggy will jackknife at about 45 degrees whereas a cart can turn 360 degrees and follow the movement of the horse.

Now we have our Roadster ready for his first show, and from now on all that is necessary is practice, much showing, and putting a "finish" on the horse. He should improve his technique (as will you) after a few shows under his belt, and then settle down to a show ring career with great enthusiasm. From time to time it may be necessary to go back a few steps and re-train a particular point, or to correct some habit that is forming, but for the most part what is needed is practice and lots of work.

Roadster Horse in bike. "Grand Prix" Champion Roadster owned and driven by William Blacklaw, Singing Hills Stable, Oregon City, Oregon.

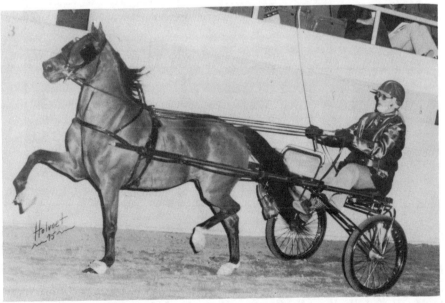

Roadster Pony in bike. "Little Cora," Hackney Road Pony, owned and driven by Barry Blacklaw, Singing Hills Stable, Oregon City, Oregon.

Roadster Horse to a road wagon. "Star Lee Over," winning the Roadster Stake at the Royal Winter Fair. Owned and driven by Mr. Ralph E. Walker, Walkerton, Ontario. This horse was Champion at the Royal in 1974, 1975, and 1976.

Roadster pair to a road wagon. "Star Lee Over" and "Miss Jeanie-B" winning the Canadian National Exhibition 1976. Owned and driven by Mr. Ralph Walker, Walkerton, Ontario. This pair won at the Royal Winter Fair in 1975 and 1976.

9
The American Saddle Horse

The American Saddle Horse has often been called "The Horse America Made" and "The All-American Horse", because of his development by the pioneer horsemen of Kentucky. He was developed mainly in the states of Virginia, Carolina and Kentucky as the answer to the tremendous need for a comfortable riding horse. These states carried on with saddle horses long after other states had taken up the British style of trotting horses in harness. The Saddle Horse owes his lineage to many breeds, each of which contributed their own specialty to the new breed. First of these contributors was the famed Narragansett pacer, a small, usually sorrel colored horse distinguished by both their habit of pacing and their hardiness and sureness of foot. They were much sought after for females who had to travel by horseback in those times because of their easy movements and smooth ride. Another breed that played a role in the development of the Saddle Horse was the Canadian Horse, a popular breed in Canada and the New England States whose ancestors came from the court of Louis XIV in France. These sturdy, wiry, and adaptable little animals were also noted for their ability to pace. They were equally at home under saddle or in harness. Also significant in the Saddle Horse breeding program were the Canadian horses known as Copperbottom, Tom Hal, and Old Pilot, who nicked very well with the top Saddle horses of the time. Morgans also made a great contribution to the new breed. Among the more notable were Indian Chief, Peavine, and Sherman. Their conformation and stamina played a large part in producing the quality desired in Saddle Horses. The Standardbred Horse, also in its infancy at the time, deserves a lot of credit for its contribution. Mambrino Chief, Harrison Chief, and Abdallah 1 were some of the better known sires of the day. From this melting pot of many breeds and breedings came Denmark, who won the designation of Foundation Sire. With this auspicious beginning, the American Saddle Horse Breeders Association was formed in 1891 and a Registry organized which continues to function to this day.

The American Saddlebred Horse has a distinguished appearance, at once distinctive and recognizable. His high well-shaped head, alert ears, expressive and wide-set eyes mark him immediately as an aristocrat. He usually has a long, well-arched neck that tapers to a fine throat latch, set high on a good withers. His shoulders are sloping, indicating great freedom of movement in front, and his withers are well-defined. He should have a short back, level croup, and tail coming out high up. He has powerful hind quarters that are muscular and well-developed, straight legs, and long sloping pasterns to provide the springiness necessary for a smooth comfortable gait. He is a closely knit horse with no chunkiness about him. His whole appearance is one of elegance.

The average height of the Saddle Horse is 15 to 16 hands and the weight from 1,000 to 1,200 pounds. He is a courageous, spirited horse with a coat that is both beautiful and glossy and a temperament that is docile and intelligent.

The American Saddlebred Horse is shown in harness in several classes. He is shown in combination classes under the 3-gaited section which means that he shows first in harness, then under saddle as a 3-gaited horse. The requirements for this class are that he is to be shown to an appropriate four-wheeled vehicle at a walk and trot. He is judged on performance, quality, and manners with 50 percent of the class for harness and 50 percent under saddle. (We will not concern ourselves in this book with the saddle half.) He is also shown in Fine Harness where the requirements consist of an animated park trot and an animated walk. He is again judged on manners, quality, and performance. He must stand quietly and is not required to back. The other harness class available for Saddlebreds is the pleasure driving class. The requirements for the class are that he be shown with a full mane and tail hitched to a suitable two or four-wheeled vehicle. He is to be shown at a flat walk, park trot, and brisk trot. He must stand quietly and back readily. The class as well is judged on manners, quality, and performances

From the foregoing list of classes and their requirements we can see that each class demands a different way of going and is judged on qualifications that differ in order of importance. The harness used in each class also differs, as does the rule concerning mane and tail. We will discuss each class in turn and discover how this one breed of horse can show in such different ways.

Combination 3-Gaited Saddle Horse

The combination 3-gaited Saddle Horse shows first in harness and then under saddle. Each half of the class counts 50 percent. Showing in harness, the Saddlebred displays his proud bearing to advantage and combines an animated high, clean trot with elegance and beauty. The 3-gaited horse is shown with roached mane and tail, and the tail is usually set and held in a high arc. This is utilized to set off his well-developed quarters and display his good hock action to best advantage. He is characterized by a high and proud head carriage which is achieved easily with his neck length, fine throat latch, and high elegant tail set. His action is high and snappy with good reach, and with such a long, sloping shoulder he has the utmost freedom of movement in his stride. He seems to float around the ring with effortless and tireless dignity, maintaining a cheerful and alert personality at all times. The Saddlebred usually wears a fair weight of shoe and carries a long toe, the combination of which produces the distinctive action so long associated with the breed. His action behind is equally good since his powerful hock action gives tremendous impulsion and creates the momentum for the elegance in front.

The combination horse is required to show at a walk and trot both ways of the ring. He is judged on performance, quality, and manners. One attendant is permitted in the ring to head the horse in the lineup. Here the horse should be well-mannered and stand quietly. If asked to back, he should do so freely with head set and under control—he must never rush off in reverse with head thrown up and obviously out of control.

The walk of the Saddlebred should be animated, graceful, true, and straight. It should be a very springy gait—a four beat cadence with impulsion emanating from behind and a high, elegant action in front. He should "pick them up and set them down" with obvious vigor and determination; sluggishness, disinterest or sourness should never be associated with this breed or this gait. The walk should be true and straight—two qualifications that are very important and sometimes overlooked by a trainer. His feet should lift and fall perpendicularly, not arc or wing out to one side, and he should not describe "S" curves as he travels. Shoeing will help in this respect, as balance is affected very quickly by improper shoeing or weights.

The trot called for in a Combination 3-gaited Saddlebred class is the park trot. This designates a high action two-beat gait with great animation, presence, and vitality. The front knees should come up high describing a snappy arc, and the legs should fold under rhythmically and with great elegance. The head is held very high, allowing the horse to really get up there, and the powerful hind quarters deliver tremendous impulsion to produce animation and verve. The horse should have really good hock action as well as knee action in front and should be balanced and capable of handling himself at this medium speed with brilliance. Brilliance, elegance, and graceful rhythm are the keynotes of this eye-catching class.

Equipment

In keeping with the fine characteristics of the horse, the harness used in the Combination class is a fine and elegant one. The bridle has a considerable amount of patent leather as does all of the harness, and has certain requisites as to type. It must have side checks, round blinkers, and a curb type of bit, usually a liverpool. The check bit is usually a straight bar snaffle with small rings. The bridle should have box loop cheeks, a fine noseband, and finely shaped buckles. The breast collar is usually the folded and sewn style with patent leather overlay, and buckled on traces, which are sometimes made round or beaded back to the flat ends. The neck strap, which is very fine, is sometimes made round and has a hold back tab. No martingale is used in this class. The backpad is patent leather right around and usually mounted on a spring steel tree these days. The bellyband is of soft folded and sewn style, finely made shaft loops of open style, wrap straps of not more than 5/8", and rein terrets of very fine round type. The crupper can be buckled or sewn on, and the crupper strap should be fine, no more than 5/8" thick. The reins may be black with tan handparts or all russett, and sometimes are either beaded or made round to the handparts. They should have steel ends where they buckle onto the bit. Hardware throughout should be solid brass, and as fine as is practical. Breeching is not worn.

The vehicle used in this class is usually the Fine Harness show buggy or a similar one. It does not have to be a side-bar type; ordinary springing front and rear is quite acceptable. It should be a light, showy, well-appointed buggy in keeping with the elegance displayed by the horse and harness. It usually has a patent leather dash, chromed seat railing, and a highly polished finish with maroon or wine colored carpet and cushion.

Training

The Saddlebred is started the same way as are the other breeds, and by the end of his basic training (outlined in Chapter I) is ready to go into serious advanced training for the Combination class. He should already be well balanced, obedient, responsive, and capable. If that is the case, we can go about producing the finish required for the show ring. Great consideration must be given to his shoeing and foot length as this is used in close conjunction with the training methods. With his career in mind, the latter few months of his basic training should have seen the growth of a good foot and the first weighted shoes. He must be accustomed to both and capable of handling his legs with them before advanced training can be seriously begun.

As the walk is a difficult gait to achieve, we will begin with the trot. We are trying to achieve great animation, collection, and high action from our combination prospect, and the trot is the easiest place to start. It is much easier for the horse to put animation and impulsion into a trot at the beginning than it is at a walk where he tends to relax. Our basic training was done with relaxation and confidence in mind so that the horse was encouraged to do everything quietly and calmly. Now, however, we want to excite him a bit and produce vigor and vitality in his movements and attitude. It must be done in a sensible way in order not to either confuse or frighten him. Scare tactics should never be used to produce animation and impulsion because eventually the horse would become a nervous wreck and useless for any purpose.

As we trot on the rail, we begin to demand more impulsion from our horse. As we restrain him, he is urged to ever greater amounts of animation and output. Most likely, his checkrein has been raised a hole already. As we drive it should be inspected regularly for results— whether or not it is doing the job of raising not only the horse's head, but his whole front end. We will no doubt have to experiment considerably with the length of checkrein in conjunction with other aids to arrive at optimum length. Initially, it should not be raised too much, as the young horse has to learn gradually to handle himself at the new animated gait as well as adjust to the new higher head carriage. Never change several pieces of harness adjustment at once; not only will you be uncertain which pieces is causing which result, but the horse cannot adapt to too many changes at once. Our advance training must be every bit as methodical and step-by-step as was our basic training if we are to achieve the finished product we would like to see.

As more and higher action is achieved, make sure the horse is keeping his form and style and really working off his hocks. Be careful not to sacrifice the action of the hind quarters to achieve knee action in front. To this end, we deep driving on continually from the hind end as we take back in front. The horses' action can be improved at this point by the use of rattlers in either the wooden balls or light chain style. The rattlers should be fitted on only the front feet to start with in order to accustom the horse to their action. The horse should be driven from the ground initially. Once he has accepted them, he should be hitched and driven off immediately. Never allow a horse to slouch or jog along slowly and quietly when wearing rattlers. He should learn to associate them with vivacity, animation, and a "going on" gait—we are trying to develop his action to a greater degree, which cannot be done at the slow flat gaits. Rattlers may be used on all four feet if the hind action also needs some improvement. The horse should be driven well up into his bit and encouraged to considerable effort and animation. A good firm contact should be maintained at the park trot, with many releases in between, such as if one was squeezing a sponge. A solid, steady pull will only destroy the effect of your hands because the horse's mouth will become numb and immune to pressure. This light but firm support comes with practice, and care must be taken that the little squeezes are just that and not pulls. You can usually tell by observing the reaction of the horse's head to these motions. He will jerk his head up if the effect is too strong and abrupt. On the other hand, the very firm support is necessary to maintain gait and cadence; otherwise the trot will degenerate into too much speed with less of action and form. Lightness of hand will produce that beautiful effect of effortless elegance that is desired in a Saddlebred in harness.

As we train for the park trot we should intersperse our work on the rail with halts in the center as well as practicing at the parked position. Saddlebreds should be stretched somewhat to display their conformation to better advantage. This should be taught at home using voice commands so that the attendant does not need to stand the horse on his feet forcibly. It takes very little time for the horse to associate lining up with a parked out position. Use the same voice command each time (whether it be "stretch", "stand out", or whatever) as the attendant moves the front feet out into position either by tapping the leg behind the fetlock or pastern or manually lifting it up and out. It will not take many sessions for this to become a habit. Soon the horse will begin to settle his hind feet together immediately upon halting in the lineup and then, with a bit of encouragement such a shake of the reins or a slight ripple sent up to his mouth, he will move his front feet out into the desired position. This looks very efficient in the show ring and is more desirable than having him forcibly stood up and re-stood up as he moves out of parked position or fidgets. The stretched position keeps a horse from fussing and moving around in lineup and often prompts the horse to stand straighter all over. This parked out stance was developed at the beginning of the breed's history not only to make the horse look pretty but to ensure his standing quietly while ladies mounted and dismounted. In order to move off, the horse has to step his feet into position underneath him. This takes only an instant but is sufficient time for mounting or leaving the carriage.

Now that we have our Combination horse performing well at the park trot, we can ask him to do an animated walk. Bring him down from a trot to the walk, keeping him well collected. He should be pushed on enough to retain impulsion and vigor, yet maintain a four-beat walk. The walk should be springy and free, covering ground satisfactorily with good action all around. Head and neck should be high and flexed, ears alert, and the horse should exude an attitude of keeness. The walk must never degenerate to a "stroll through the pasture" type of gait. The gait should be elastic and animated. Hind legs should be stepping well under the horse with each stride and be straight and true. Push your horse on until this effect is achieved, holding him back enough to keep him from breaking into a trot. Constant squeezing and releasing of the reins combined with encouraging clucks will produce the impulsion necessary to channel into the energetic quick-striding walk desired.

Practice transitions from the walk to the park trot, as this should be done smoothly. With your horse collected and walking with great ambition and animation, cluck him on. Give him more rein as you do and the trot should result. All that is necessary then is to send him on and up into his bridle and set him at the speed desired. Transitions downward from park trot to the walk should also be practiced so that it can be done without awkwardness or loss of form.

The headset of your combination horse is very important and the use of a bitting rig once or twice a week will help produce the desired height and set. The bitting rig may be adjusted in several ways and should be varied occasionally to keep the horse from becoming bored or too accustomed to it. A good beginning is to run a solid rein from one side of the bit through the checkrein loop on the backpad and on to the other side of the bit. Adjust this rein tight enough to place the horse's head almost in the position desired, but not so tight that he cannot get relief by tucking. His tucking action to slacken the rein will lengthen the muscle on top of his neck. With continued use this headset will become a natural position for him. A good practice is to put him in the bitting rig for twenty to thirty

Combination Saddle Horse in show buggy. "Carberry's Lyric," 16:1 hands, owned, trained, and shown to an undefeated career by Mrs. Celia Lundy, Vancouver, B.C. "Lyric" was high point horse in the Saddlebred division at the Pacific National Exhibition for six consecutive years.

Combination Saddle Horse under saddle. "Carberry's Lyric," now retired, undefeated. Owned and shown by Mrs. Celia Lundy, Vancouver, B.C.

minutes, then take him straight out and drive him in harness with your hands simulating the action of the rein of the bitting rig. He will thus learn to "give" to your hands the way he does to the bitting rig. A variation is to cross the side reins of the bitting rig over his shoulders; i.e., running the side rein from the left side of the backpad over the shoulder and fastening on to the right side of the bit and vice versa for the right rein. The bitting rig can also be used in the conventional manner by using the side checks through the drops on the bridle crown and the side reins running straight to the bit (see chapter 2).

Your Combination horse is now ready to show in the harness half of the class and needs only practice in an actual show to perfect his technique.

Fine Harness Horse

A Fine Harness horse is usually a bit heavier and stronger than a 3-gaited horse. The nature of his work, especially when shown in a 5-gaited class requires more strength and endurance. Fine Harness horses are extremely brilliant, beautiful, and full of presence. Their long flowing manes and tails, high, proud head carriage, tremendous action, and obvious enjoyment of their work make them a most thrilling class to watch. Fine Harness horses show at a park trot and an animated walk. The park trot is a very animated, high-actioned gait of medium speed that displays the form and physique of the horse to the utmost. Although extreme speed is penalized, this horse does not need great speed to perform his elegant and breathtaking trot to best advantage. Working well off his hocks, he performs his high reaching trot with almost effortless ease. Meanwhile his long sloping shoulder gives complete freedom to front end motion. The Fine Harness horse wears quarter boots on his front feet. These add greatly to the overall picture because their startling white color defines so clearly the height and style of the horse's action. The Fine Harness horse wears a long mane and tail. The forelock and very front piece of his mane are braided with colored ribbon. This flies gaily in the wind created by his going and adds to the already beautiful picture. His tail is usually either set or a brace worn with false top tail. The brace is part of a specially designed crupper; the false top tail laces over and on to it, falling down to mingle with the real tail. Usually the false top tail is a match for his own tail color-wise. The high head carriage balanced by the high tail carriage creates a delightful symmetry and a picture that is worthy of the Fine Harness Horse.

One attendant is allowed to head the horse in a Fine Harness class, and the horse is not required to back. The horse usually stands slightly stretched or square. He should display good manners in a lineup and not fidget, fuss, or back into other entries.

Equipment

The harness worn in this class is an extremely fine, light, showy harness with considerable patent leather and solid brass fittings. The bridle has overdraw checkrein with check bit, snaffle bit, square blinkers, and either noseband or caveson. The breast collar is folded and sewn with raised patent leather layer, buckled on traces, either round or beaded traces with flat ends, narrow neck strap with hold back tab, running martingale with round or fancy narrow forks, backpad with patent leather all around (usually built on a spring steel tree), and shaft loops of open style. The bellyband has fine wrap straps, the crupper is of sewn on or buckled on style usually with built in metal brace, and reins either black with tan handparts, and made round or beaded back to that part or all russet. Hand holds are allowed, but as good manners are essential they are not desirable. Breeching is not worn.

The vehicle used for this class is the Fine Harness show buggy, a very light and fancy four-wheeled side-bar buggy with patent leather trim on dash and apron, and a very good finish on the woodwork. Chrome abounds on this buggy, and the carpet and cushion are usually of maroon or deep wine color. The shafts are light and fine, made of second growth hickory and finished beautifully as is the buggy itself. Quite often a contrasting pin striping effect is incorporated into the finish and the overall picture of horse, harness, and buggy is one of extreme elegance and beauty.

Classes

The usual classes for this type of horse are as follows: Junior Fine Harness horse, which is judged on quality, performance, and manners in that order of importance; Fine Harness horse, ladies, junior exhibitors, amateurs, owners, amateur owners, which is judged on manners, quality, and performance; and Fine Harness Horse, which is judged on performance, quality, and manners. We can clearly see from these requirements of judging that all Fine Harness classes are judged on the same qualifications, but in different orders of importance depending upon classification. In all classes, the same gaits are required; the "park trot," "walk," and "show your horse." The latter command means that the driver should show his entry to his best advantage while recalling excessive speed will be penalized. "Show your horse" is never given in classes for ladies, junior exhibitors, amateurs, or amateur owners.

Training

The training for the Fine Harness class follows the same lines as those described for the Combination Horse. From his basic training he is gradually checked higher and asked for increasing animation and impulsion while he is restrained gently to a proper speed. His action will not be as trappy as the Combination horse; he has more reach and power in his stride, but this will develop out of the same type of training. It is the nature of the Fine Harness horse to be born with this brilliant and graceful ability and fortunately training will bring it out with very little prompting.

Quarter boots are worn on the horse as we train him, or rattlers can also be used if their resulting action is more desirable. Only quarter boots may be worn in the show ring, but for our training sessions we can use whatever works best for the situation at hand. As we push him on asking for ever more action and animation, we will discover the best position for his checkrein by experimentation. His naturally high head carriage dictates a high checked position, but if too tight, it will ewe his neck and some freedom of motion will be lost. He must be able to use and flex his neck to provide the balanced form so necessary to the elegance of his trot. Care must be taken to see that he always works off his hocks and that he uses his hocks well. Good hock action is very desirable in this class.

Once the park trot is established fairly well, we can slow our horse down to an animated walk. This is achieved by keeping him up to the bit as he is pushed along, while still restraining him to a graceful tempo. The walk should be vivacious and elastic with good action all around, and demonstrate even and regular cadence. He should not hop, skip, and vary his beat constantly. Rather he should go straight without winging or paddling and his walk should cover some ground. He should maintain an alert and keen look, never showing sour ears or having to be constantly pushed on in an obvious manner. He should seem to enjoy his own performance!

The head set of the Fine Harness horse is very important. A bitting rig is a most useful piece of equipment to assist in this matter because with proper adjustment the head can be set in any position desired and trained to carry that way. Care and gentleness must be used because the side reins and side checks can be adjusted in a most uncomfortable position that after a period of time will become downright painful to the horse. When used properly, however, they serve to assist in the setting of the horse's head to a great degree. A dumb jockey can also be used if more elevation and a different position is necessary. This deviation from the ordinary bitting rig is simply a pole mounted on the backpad with rings positioned up about a foot to which the side reins, side checks, and crupper strap may be attached (and which changes the "controls" for the horse). When used on the lounge line good results may occur. Remember that animation and speed control may also be practiced at the same time. The bitting rig must be used with a straight bar bit—not a jointed one—or the horse's mouth will be hurt. It should not be left on for long periods of time, either; twenty minutes on the lunge line is sufficient for a lesson. Used once or twice a week, the bitting rig is a real asset to the training program.

In classes calling for "show your horse", the driver is able to ask his horse for literally everything he has. He shoves him on, asking for even greater impulsion behind and instead of letting it result in much more speed, he channels it into higher and more spectacular action. In short bursts of incredible animation he demonstrates the tremendous capabilities of the Fine Harness horse in action. This gait is a wonderful crowd pleaser and the spectators react with cheers, claps, and noisy foot thumpings—all of which spur the horse on to even greater efforts. In view of this, the horse should be subjected to some of this type of noise at home during his advanced training. Have some friends clap and cheer noisily as you drive and accustom the horse to this side of his new show career. He will be more likely to perform better if he has an inkling of what is to happen. Loud cheering and clapping can be terrifying to a young horse under strange and exciting conditions if he has no previous experience. On the other hand, he will likely perform with more vim and vigor when excited, so once he is accustomed to noise it may enhance his performance rather than detract from it.

Some work should be done on the proper position in a lineup. The horse should stand either square or slightly stretched. He can easily learn this at home as you give him a breather between work outs on the rail. One attendant is permitted in the ring to head the horse and stand him on his feet, but if the horse can achieve this position unaided so much the better. A Fine Harness horse is not required to back up but he is required to show manners and stand quietly. Consequently, he should be made to stand for fairly long periods at home lined up and set up and be reprimanded every time he moves.

Fine Harness horse in Show Buggy. "Peavine's Magic Affair," owned and driven by Mrs. Wm. Blacklaw, Singing Hills Stable, Oregon City, Oregon.

Pleasure Driving Saddlebred Horse

When shown in the Pleasure Driving class, the American Saddlebred is a different temperment of animal than either the 3-gaited or Fine Harness horse. The Pleasure horse must be above all else, a pleasure to drive and handle. He is shown at a flat walk, park trot, and brisk trot and must stand quietly and back readily. He may be shown to either a two-wheeled cart or a four-wheeled buggy, but the type must be specified by the show committee. The class is judged on manners, quality, and performance. Quarter boots are *not* allowed in this class and an extremely high action is not required.

This class requires the driver to be either an amateur or a junior exhibitor. This gives the driver a break since he will not have to compete with the professionals who dominate the other two driving classes. Stallions are not allowed in the pleasure driving class, which makes the class more relaxing and pleasant for a beginner to participate.

Horses in this class are shown with full mane and tail, which must be carried naturally. The tail must not be gingered or put in a tail set in preparation for the show. A horse whose tail has at one time been set is not excluded, however, as long as the tail is no longer worn in a tail set.

The Pleasure Driving horse will display a good square trot without great animation, but with impulsion and obvious keenness indicating the intention to "go somewhere". His action should be the natural high and airy action which is the trademark of the breed. However, this should be accomplished without heavy shoes and extremely long toes. His gait should be springy, well cadenced, and comfortable looking. The park trot is a medium speed trot wherein the horse moves smoothly and works with his hind legs well under him to produce a free, airy action in front. His knee action should be well defined without that extreme height and snap associated with the Fine Harness horse, and his legs should fold under in a truth rhythm. He should trot well on the diagonals, with his long springy pasterns absorbing the landings of each footfall in a smooth and pleasing manner. He should carry his head well-flexed at a good height and should have excellent mouth manners. He must never pull, toss his head, go sideways resisting the bit, or throw up his head and speed off. His whole demeanor must be one of a Pleasure type of driving horse. He should carry a gay, natural tail and have good balance and responsiveness.

The brisk trot is somewhat faster than the park trot, but excessive speed is neither desired or required. The Pleasure horse should be able to move on and produce a good road-covering trot when it is demanded of him. He must retain his form at the faster trot and continue to work well off his hocks, but must never string out behind or lose his cadence. On the corners he must bend into his turns and not side rein, nor should he turn his head to the outside. He should be easily controlled at all speeds, a factor to consider since manners are paramount in this class.

The walk of the Pleasure Driving horse should be flatfooted and of a true four-beat cadence. He should not mince along or hop, skip, and mix the gaits, but rather continue in a straight line at a springy, elastic, and rapid walk keeping his form constantly.

In the lineup, the Pleasure Driving horse is required to stand quietly and without an attendant at his head. He should display a quiet sensible manner without fuss or head tossing. He should be stretched slightly, and when asked to back should do so with ease and willingness. Always remember to step a stretched horse one step forward before asking him to back up so that he can regain his balance. After a few steps backwards he should walk calmly into the lineup and once more set himself up in the proper stance.

Equipment

The harness worn by the Pleasure Driving horse should be a light showy harness with snaffle bit. Either overdraw checkrein or side checks may be used in conjunction with the snaffle bit. A light, fine breast collar is worn, of either folded and sewn style or flat leather one piece design. This is usually accompanied by a running martingale. The traces may be either sewn on or buckled on and need not be made round or beaded for that extra fancy look seen in the Fine Harness class. The backpad usually has patent leather on the top pad itself, but the panels need not be patent all the way around. Open shaft loops are used, and bellyband with wrap straps is preferred. The crupper is sewn on and the crupper strap is fairly narrow. Brass hardware is preferable, but good solid nickel or chrome fittings may be used if desired. Reins are black back to the hand parts, which are of tan leather. Hand holds are unnecessary and should be discouraged in a pleasure class. Breeching is not worn in this class. Quarter boots are not allowed in a Pleasure Driving class.

The vehicle used in this class can be either a two-wheeled cart or a four-wheeled show buggy. Whichever type is to be used should be designated in the prize list by the show committee. If a two-wheeled cart is to be used, one that is in good proportion size-wise should be obtained. Chromed wheels, a good paint job and nice upholstery adds to the overall picture of neatness and tidiness. The harness should be adjusted so that the shafts are not on too much of an angle upwards since this destroys both the balance of the cart and the pleasing proportions. If this angle cannot be made less steep, the cart is too small for the horse. Bearings, fittings and all nuts and bolts should be checked regularly for safety's sake, as a broken part can cause an accident in a crowded show ring.

If a four-wheeled show buggy is considered, the Pleasure Driving horse can use either a regular Fine Harness Buggy or a similar show buggy with regular springing arrangement instead of the side rails. Either one will handle the same way and look equally pleasing behind the horse. A good deal of chrome on a show buggy looks quite nice and adds glamour to any class. The buggy should always be well polished and neatly turned out. Again, all parts should be checked regularly, especially wheel nuts because these can work loose in a rough ring very quickly with disastrous results.

Training

For this class, our young colt is already very well suited with his extensive basic training. Since this class is a pleasure class, it does not demand the tremendous amount of animation and brilliance which require the horse be worked up to "concert pitch." The Pleasure horse is expected to perform in a pleasurable manner and to be easily handled and fun to drive.

Our colt already has this ability and needs only some actual practice in a show ring with the noise and excitement to perfect his abilities. If he is a bit lazy in front, it will be of value to use rattlers for awhile to increase action. He should be sent on firmly if it becomes necessary to use them, but this breed of horse is seldom lazy by nature and usually doesn't require this added improvement. Care must be taken not to produce a stilted and choppy up-and-down type of action in front—this is not what we wish to see in a Pleasure Driving horse. Freedom of movement coupled with a good knee action and strong hocks will result in a smooth looking, airy, floating trot that gives the impression the horse could continue all day.

With the regulations allowing either overdraw or side check rein, the trainer should choose whichever one works best with his particular horse. A horse with an upright, muscular and arched neck usually looks and goes better in a side check style of checkrein, while a horse with a long tapering neck will probably perform best in an overdraw checkrein. The trainer should experiment with both to decide which will give him the best performance and allow him to make the most use of his horse's abilities. Head set plays such an important part in a horse's way of going that all efforts possible should be made to achieve the optimum height and angle. A horse that constantly wants to poke his nose out and ewe his neck may work much better in a side check type of bridle and will give rather than resist the bit. On the other hand, there are horses that tend to overbend easily and these might be easier to set properly with an overdraw checkrein.

For the park trot, send the horse on at a good clip and then take him back to produce some collection and a good rhythmic cadence. This will give a nice height of knee action without a restricted look and at the same time prevent sprawling or stringing out with the hind end. As momentum is lost, but before he "runs down," send him on again and take him back in the same manner. In this way the performance can be continued round after round with no erratic steps or variance of speed. Support the horse well on his corners in case he begins to turn his head outward, using little half halts on the inside rein to keep his head where it should be.

The brisk trot evolves out of the park trot and is slightly faster. When you send him on, do not take him back quite so much. The result will be more speed but with the same good cadence and form. As he trots smartly along, his head carriage should be steady; it must not swing from side to side nor should he toss it. His tail carriage is important, too, and should be carried at good elevation with a gay look. He should not switch his tail—this is considered a fault.

The walk should be flatfooted, a distinct four-beat cadence done in a rapid, springy, straight manner. Good contact should be kept with the horse's mouth at the walk but not a heavy pull or constant jobbing of his mouth. Just enough feel on the lines should be exerted to keep him up to his bit and walking up smartly; he should not be allowed to slouch or jig along. While he should be fairly relaxed at this gait, he should not be asleep or have to be constantly pushed on. Practice coming down from the park trot to the walk and keeping him into a smart beat for a round or two, then back into the trot. In this way he will not become bored or have the chance to mope along. A good walk is very essential in a pleasure horse because a great deal of his actual work outside of the show ring will be done at that gait.

Work should be done in lining up squarely and practicing the required stance. He should be taught to stretch upon command. This can be accomplished by having a helper move his feet out into position as you tell him "stretch" (or a similar command), and shake the reins slightly. Very soon all that will be necessary when stopped in a lineup will be the slight shake of the lines. If you are using a four-wheeled buggy it is absolutely essential that you line up straight, otherwise when you have to back up the front wheels will jackknife on approximately the second step backward.

When teaching the back up, after making sure the four wheels are lined up straight, ask the colt to back one step at a time with the pull and release system. In this way small corrections can be made when necessary. Because of his anatomy a horse backs up first one direction then the other—both very slight deviations from the straight line but enough so that if the buggy is crooked to begin with a problem will appear almost immediately. This is where absolute control is necessary—even to the point of regulating the length of his stride. By pulling harder we get a longer step backward and with a very light pull and instant release we get a short step. A great deal of practice is necessary to become competent at this system. Backing in a two-wheeled cart is no problem since our colt has already been taught this maneuver in his basic training.

10
THE APPALOOSA HORSE

The Appaloosa horse, a name derived from the Palouse River in Washington, is a breed that was very highly prized by the Nez Pierce Indians for their toughness, endurance, and color. The most obvious feature of the Appaloosa, according to the Appaloosa historian Dr. Francis Haines, is the white rump on the rear half of the animal which resembles a patch of newly fallen snow. This patch contains several symmetrical spots of color which on different animals may range from buckskin to black. The hair on these darker spots is of a finer texture and is thicker than the rest of the coat. The skin beneath each spot is black. On the preferred type of Appaloosa the spots are round or oval and measure from one to four inches on the short axis. Also characteristic is part-colored skin noticeable around the mouth, eyes, nostrils, and genitals. The ideal Appaloosa horse would be around 15 hands and weigh at least 1,000 pounds.

The blanket pattern is not the only one for an Appaloosa horse; there are at least six different patterns of markings and dozens of variations and combinations. Some are white with dark spots over the entire body while others are a mottling of dark and white with dark areas about the frontal bones, jowls, neck, hip bone, and stifle. Hoof markings often show vertical stripes or else are parti-colored black and white.

The general appearance of the Appaloosa should be symmetrical and smooth. The head should be straight with parti-colored skin about the nostrils and lips. The sclera of the eye is white, giving the eye some prominence. The neck should show quality and have a clean cut throat latch, and the chest should be deep and blend into long, well-muscled sloping shoulders. The withers should be well-defined and prominent and the back should be short and straight. The loin is short and wide and the underline should be long. Legs should be muscular and straight with medium length of sloping pastern. Hooves are striped, rounded, deep and wide at the heels.

In harness the Appaloosa makes a very colorful turnout. His quiet, sensible, tractable disposition make him an ideal pleasure driving horse and he takes to the harness work readily. In the show ring the Appaloosa is shown in Pleasure Driving and in Buckboard Pleasure Driving. For these classes, the mane may be natural or roached and the tail should be trimmed to fall near or above the hocks. There is no stipulation regarding braiding—this is left up to the individual and if he or she feels like braiding the horse, it is permissable to do so. There is no definite foot length, but extreme length of foot or extreme high action can be penalized by a judge. Standard horse shoes are prescribed, therefore weighted shoes would be prohibited.

Attendants are not allowed in the ring to head the horses in the line up and Appaloosas are not required to be stretched. Horses should stand square and straight.

Appaloosa Pleasure Driving Class

In this class the horse is to be shown to a suitable two or four-wheeled vehicle, type of which is optional to the show committee but must be specified in the prize list. The horse is shown at a flatfooted walk, a slow trot, and a fast trot. He is required to stand quietly and back readily. The class is judged on manners, quality, and performance.

Appaloosa Buckboard Pleasure Driving Class

In this class either one or two horses are shown as a pleasure horse to a four-wheel buckboard or suitable antique four-wheeled vehicle. The type of vehicle is optional providing it portrays an early American or frontier mode of transportation. The horse or horses are to be shown at a flatfooted walk, a slow trot, and a fast trot. The horses must work both directions of the ring, stand quietly in the lineup, and back readily. This class is judged 50 percent manners, equipment, and performance, 30 percent on conformation, quality, 10 percent on suitability to purpose, and 10 percent on uniformity of entry, neatness, and originality of attire.

Harness

In both of the above driving classes, a standard light set of driving harness is called for unless, of course, the old-fashioned vehicle being used in the buckboard class is a very heavy one. In that case a heavier type of harness would be necessary. The harness should match the vehicle in this respect. The light set of single harness will include a bridle and the rules are such that either an overdraw checkrein or side check type may be used. It may be used in conjunction with either a snaffle bit or a liverpool bit, depending upon the individual needs of the horse. The bridle may have blinkers or be used as an open bridle—again, the choice is left up to the driver. The breast collar should be a serviceable weight, about 2½ inches, and sewn on traces are more practical than the buckled on style. The backpad should be of good width, about 3 inches, and while a patent leather top is certainly prettier than the plain leather, it is not a necessity. The bellyband should have wrap straps and the crupper should be the sewn on style. Spoon cruppers are prohibited for Appaloosa driving classes. Breeching is optional, but if the vehicle being used is at all heavy it should be added to the harness. Reins should be black with tan hand parts, and hardware can be either nickel or brass. Harness, whatever type being used, should always be clean, neat, and absolutely sound.

If a pair of horses (often called a team) is to be used to pull the vehicle, the harness used will be of different style . . . collar and hames will be more in keeping with the era of the class than breast collar style, but either may be used. If collar and hames are used, the collars must fit properly. When on the horse's neck, the four fingers of one hand must be able to be inserted between his neck and the bottom of the collar. The collars must also be wide enough at the draft for the neck. Any type of collar may be used from a Kay type (which is usually considered a show collar) to the buckle on work style. The latter, which open at the top and buckle to close, are easier to put on and fit and more likely to match the vintage of the vehicle being used.

The hames can also be of several types; the one most in keeping with the turnout should be used. The fine show style metal hames usually go with the Kay type collar, and the heavier metal or wooden hames suit the buckle on collars much better. The hames also must fit properly on the collar and are secured top and bottom with a hame strap. Light backpads are used on a pair with slots for the traces to run through, and a comfortable width of bellyband. Crupper straps and cruppers are of standard pattern. A breastplate is usually considered a part of pair harness. It serves to keep the collar in place by buckling around the bottom of it and hence to the bellyband. The bridles are of plain leather, either with or without blinkers, and often without any checkreins at all. The bits can be snaffle type or liverpool, or any type that works best with the horses being used. There is no stipulation in this respect because in the era being depicted many types of bits were in common use. Although blinkers are not mandatory in the buckboard class, the writer highly recommends their use for safety's sake and for better performance from the horses. Horses that work quietly at home with open bridles may often see scary or exciting things in a show ring that will send them straight into a runaway or even into another buggy turnout in the ring. With blinkers, however, most of the outside effects are cut off so that they can concentrate their attention on their work. Neck yokes should be used as they were used in that period far more than the newer type of pole chains seen on fancier "gentlemen's turnouts." With the neck yokes, the pair will be equipped with pole straps which connect them from collar to neck yoke, and provide the means of backing up the rig. Breeching may also be worn, although on a light buckboard or similar weight of vehicle it is not necessary. Hip straps may also be worn and may be most useful in holding up the traces when the singletrees are mounted on a low doubletree.

Care must be taken to achieve proper adjustment of the coupling reins, as this makes or breaks the driving skill of the owner. If the pair are evenly matched for size, temperament, and way of going, the coupling reins will be put on evenly, but if one horse is bigger, keener, or differently gaited, the couplings must be adjusted to compensate for the difference. Often much experimenting is necessary before the proper lengths are found. If one horse carries his head higher than the other it will be to your advantage to put his spreader rein on top so as not to be constantly jibbing the other horse's inside rein. Coupling reins must be long enough to eliminate any fear of their going forward and being caught up by their buckles in the rein terrets.

Vehicle

In the Pleasure Driving class the vehicle used may be either two or four-wheeled. If a two-wheeled cart is used, the cross country type of wooden cart is more in keeping with the heritage of the Appaloosa than the modern metal style, but either may be used. The size of the cart should be in proportion to that of the horse. If a four-wheeled buggy is used, a fine harness show buggy will be considered correct, as will other styles of light show buggies.

A four-wheeled vehicle is stipulated in the Buckboard Pleasure Driving class. There is, however, considerable leeway in the type of buggy to be used since the only condition to be met is that the buggy must protray an early American or frontier mode of transportation. This Buckboard class was designed to depict such an era and the Appaloosa horse was a very important part of this page in history.

Whatever vehicle used should be carefully examined to make sure everything is sound and in good working condition. Wheel nuts, bolts, and nuts holding on the body and reach should be checked for looseness, and shafts must be without breaks or splits.

Training

No special training is necessary for the Pleasure Driving or Buckboard driving classes above which our colt has learned in his basic schooling. He is already driving happily, freely, and safely in a cart or buggy and no fancy or artificial gaits are required of him for the show ring. He has already been taught to walk and trot properly, to stand quietly for a good length of time, and to back up readily.

Rattlers, action chains, boots or any artificial appliances are prohibited and should never be used even in training. Indeed, there is no point in using this type of training as extreme high action is severely penalized by a judge. Set tails or gingered tails are also prohibited, as is extreme hoof length. The accent as we can see from these rules is to keep the Appaloosa natural and to show him at his natural gaits.

The walk of the Appaloosa in harness should be true, flatfooted, and energetic. He should not doddle along half heartedly, nor describe "S"-curves along the rail, but should go straight and with ground covering rhythm. His ears should be alert and his expression one of interest in his work. Sour ears and a dejected attitude are not acceptable.

The slow trot is an easy, free-moving gait, wherein the shoulders swing in a rhythm and the legs move in a true diagonal gait. The movement should appear as if the horse could keep it up all day if necessary. The horse should display good manners and a good mouth. He should not be pulling on the bit, tossing his head, switching his tail, or going sideways. He should carry a good head set and show an alert and proud bearing.

The fast trot is a brisk road gait, but extreme speed is not desired. The horse should maintain smoothness, balance, cadence, and form while executing a good brisk trot. He should use his hocks well and move out freely in front. He should not break into a canter nor appear to be difficult or strong to control at this speed. He must go into his corners without side reining and not fall in on the turns with his quarters.

In the lineup the horse should stand square and not stretched. He must stand alone without an attendant at his head, and back readily and freely when requested to do so.

Appointments

In the Buckboard class, the judging is based on authenticity of equipment, attire of drivers, markings, and colorful qualities of horses—the overall picture and presentation is considered. No more than four people are allowed to ride in the vehicle and those who do should take care to suit their costumes to the era of the vehicle.

Pair Appaloosa horses to an old-fashioned wagon.

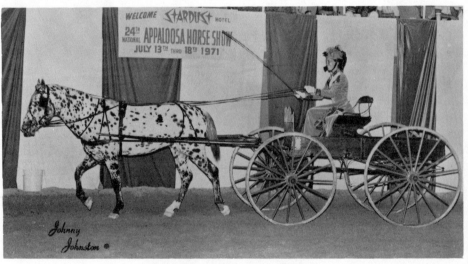

Appaloosa horse in Buggy.

11
THE PINTO HORSE

The Pinto horse derives its name from the Spanish "pintado", meaning painted, and refers to all color patterned horses. The pinto coloring is believed to be the result of the combined actions of albinism (whiteness), melanism (blackness), and erythema (redness) of the skin.

The Pinto arrived in America with the Conquistadores and once here, the unique camouflage characteristics of their coat appealed greatly to the American Indian. Indeed, some tribes painted even more spots and splashes of color whenever the horse showed too much solid white.

Pintos come in two recognized patterns: Tobiano and Overo. The Tobiano predominates in North America, Europe, and Asia while the Overo is usually seen in South America. The Tobiano pinto appears to be white with large spots of color, often overlapping on horses with a greater percentage of color than white. Spots of color typically originate from the head, chest, flank, and buttocks, often including the tail. Its legs are generally white, giving the appearance of a white horse with spots of color. The Overo Pinto appears to be a colored horse with white markings. These spots of white appear to be jagged and originate on the animal's side or belly, spreading toward the neck, tail, legs, and back. Color appears to frame the white spots. Thus an Overo often has a dark tail, mane, legs, and backline. A bald or white face often accompanies an Overo pattern.

Pintos are divided into three distinct conformation types: The stock type, the pleasure type, and the saddlebred type. The stock type is a western type horse of Quarter and Thoroughbred type, well-muscled yet refined, and possessing the conformation qualities necessary for standard western working events. The pleasure type is a horse of medium size and build who is refined and has a balanced appearance. Pleasure type Pintos reflect the conformation associated with Arabian, Morgan, and Thoroughbred breeding, and are useful in any type of event. The saddlebred type is a horse of high head carriage with the animated, high action of Saddlebred and Hackney type. This horse should be refined, with balanced, lofty carriage and conformation with the action and appearance necessary for the standard gaited and parade type events. The pleasure and saddle type Pintos are the two categories which best fit into the driving classes.

In harness the Pinto may be shown as a Formal Driving Horse, a Pleasure Driving horse, or a Roadster. The Formal Driving horse, or Fine Harness horse, would suit the saddle horse type of Pinto admirably, while the Pleasure Driving horse calls more for the Pleasure type Pinto.

The minimum height of mature Pintos eligible for registration is 14 hands. Their conformation must be sound, attractive, and show breeding quality along with performance ability. The head should be small and breedy with well-shaped ears, large alert eyes, and small muzzle. The neck should be nicely arched with well-defined throat latch, broad chest, sloping shoulders, and short back. The girth should be deep and ribs well sprung. The legs should be strong and straight with good muscles and should be set on rounded feet of medium size.

Formal Driving Class

In the Formal Driving class, the scope of sub-classes is very large including Open, Stallions, Mares, Geldings, Ladies, Amateur and Junior Exhibitors. The horses in these classes are to be shown to a suitable four-wheeled show vehicle at a walk and animated trot. They are to stand quietly in the lineup and are not required to back. The class is judged on performance, presence, manners, quality, and conformation. Horses in this class are shown with full mane and tail and a tail brace is permitted. Quarter boots or unlined bell boots are also allowed and will enhance the action of the front legs. The horses may be braided, using Saddle horse type of braiding, forelock and one braid behind the bridle path, but if an entry is not braided it will not affect his placing in the judging.

Harness

Pintos are allowed considerable variety in the regulations concerning harness. Bridles should be of light, fine showy style with box loop cheeks, patent leather blinkers, and browband. A noseband is desirable, and the

Pinto may use either overcheck or side checks for his checkrein. It is customary to use a snaffle bit with an overdraw style of checkrein. If side checks are used, they may be used in conjunction with a snaffle, liverpool, or buxton bit. Blinkers are required and may be of either round or square pattern. It is customary to use a running martingale when an overdraw checkrein is used, but this is not mandatory for the Formal Driving Class. The breast collar should be fine, no wider than 1¾ inches, and may be of either flat or folded and sewn style. The traces can be either sewn on or buckled on, but the former is stronger and safer. Although they can be beaded, a flat trace is quite satisfactory. The backpad should be fairly fine, no wider than 2½ inches, and the upper part at least should be trimmed with patent leather. Some harnesses will have the patent continuing all around; this is showier but also more costly and vulnerable. Bellyband should have fairly fine wrap straps (about ¾ inches), and the crupper may be either sewn on or buckled on, depending upon whether or not a tail brace is to be worn. Hardware should be brass if possible for such a fine harness class as this, and must be kept well polished and clean. Breeching is not worn in a Formal Driving class. Reins may be either of all russett color or black fronts with tan hand parts. Hand holds should not be necessary as the horse should be well-mannered and easily controlled without the need for such.

Vehicle

A four-wheeled show buggy is called for in this class, and the fine harness buggy is the one most commonly used. A side bar fine harness buggy is the usual style, but one sprung with ordinary leaf spring is equally acceptable. The buggy should be in show condition and gleaming with care.

Training

There will be no difficulty in bringing the colt's standard of performance up to this level of competence if the trainer has followed the training procedures outlined in chapter 1. The colt is already doing his walk and trot with ease and willingness, standing quietly for a good period of time, and backing up freely. Now begin to animate his action to achieve brilliance and finish. First, shorten his checkrein a hole or two and as you trot on the rail ask for more and more animation. This may be done by clucking him on with your voice and restraining him enough to produce height of action instead of speed. If more action is desired and he is the type able to develop such action, rattlers may be employed at the same time. Wooden rattlers or light chain anklets will produce good action and may be worn on all four pasterns. These rattlers are strictly a training device and not permitted in the show ring. Practice sending the colt on down the rail with a burst of animated enthusiasm. Then take him back for half a round and send him on again, never asking for more than he can produce. Each time he will be able to sustain the animation for a slightly longer time and will not sour but rather enjoy it as he learns what is expected of him. Make sure you work both ways of the ring equally so that the horse will not become unbalanced in one direction. The horse must work off his hocks, therefore he must be encouraged to get his legs underneath him and use his hindquarters. Shove him on and take him back, playing him enough to let him move on freely but at the same time to develop high airy action in front and good hock action behind. Once his action has developed sufficiently to ensure his balance, he should be slowed down to the proper speed required for the class. He must retain his form and balance as he trots and must be animated, cadenced, and well-collected. He has to have great impulsion from behind to obtain the high going light and airy motion in front. Do not push the colt too quickly since this type of motion requires muscling and practice, and some time must be spent in the advanced training before the desired perfection is attained. Never work him until he is tired. We want our colt to look alert, interested, and keen about his work and if we overwork him he may appear sour, uninterested, and jaded—and anything but a Formal Driving prospect!

Head set is very important, consequently some work in a bitting rig will be of advantage in this respect. Adjust the side checks and side reins to set his head where you want it to be and let him walk around his stall for fifteen or twenty minutes. Then take him straight out and lounge him with the bitting rig on. Care must be taken not to bring his head to its final set too quickly; the muscles in his neck must be gradually built up to this stage.

The walk of the Formal Driving horse must be animated—not a flat footed walk—and should be true, cadenced, and a four-beat gait. The horse must be well-collected, look brilliant, and above all must go straight! Side passing down the rail should not be permitted. It should not be a mincing, prancing gait which seems to go nowhere because an up and down on the spot is undesirable and not at all brilliant or elegant. The Pinto should walk with pride and as if he were going somewhere.

The animated trot in this class must be collected, well balanced, a true diagonal gait, and have good cadence. The horse must produce tremendous impulsion behind and be high, airy, and light in front. He must show good form at the trot and carry his head well with his chin set and ears up and keen. His whole attitude should shout of brilliance and elegance. His manners should be such that he is not pulling on the reins over much nor tossing his head, and of course he must not break gait.

Formal Driving Pinto horse. "My Foxy Lady," reg. American Saddlebred Pinto mare, owned and driven by Mr. Glenn Hepner, Surrey, B.C. at Del Mar, Calif.

Quarter boots or bell boots are usually worn in Formal Driving classes, and once your colt is performing to satisfaction, you should switch from rattlers to the quarter boots. The quarter boots must be unweighted. Their hinging motion will produce action and with the training in rattlers firmly embedded in his mind, the colt will work well in the boots. Quarter boots are more useful than bell boots in this respect, but bell boots will give good protection to the front legs if this is a problem.

If a tail brace is to be worn on the colt in the show ring, it should be fitted at home so that the colt may become accustomed to its use. Tail hair should be matched as closely as possible for color and texture.

When lined up in the center of the ring, the Pinto should stand squarely or slightly stretched, depending upon his type. If he is of Saddlebred type, he will look better stretched a bit. This training must be done at home. Each time you stop in your training ring, get out and set his feet up properly using the same command each time. Soon the colt will set himself up upon command from the buggy and you will be able to present a finished performance. The Formal Driving horse is not required to back up in the show ring.

Pinto Pleasure Driving Horses

Open, stallions, mares, geldings, Ladies, Amateur and Junior Exhibitors. This class is to be shown to a suitable two or four-wheeled vehicle. The type is optional to the show committee but must be specified in the prize list. The horses are to be shown at a flatfooted walk, a slow trot, and a fast trot. They must stand quietly and back readily. The class is judged on manners, quality, and performance.

Horses in this class may be shown with either full mane and tail or roached mane and tail. Quarter boots or bell boots are not permitted.

Harness

The harness worn in the Pleasure Driving class may be the same as that worn in the Formal Driving class or a bit less fancy. If the horse is to be shown to a fine harness buggy, he ought to wear a very fine harness to match the elegance of the turnout. However, if he is showing in a two-wheeled cart, his harness may be of a more practical nature. The bridle will be virtually the same, though perhaps not quite so fine. The exhibitor in this class has the opportunity, if he so desires, to dispense with blinkers. However, the writer would advise strongly against this idea since the blinkers add a large degree of safety to the control and management of the animal. The rule book states that blinkers are optional (though preferred) in Pleasure Driving, and unless the driver has a valid reason for using an open bridle, he should use blinkers. Again side checks or overdraw checkreins may be used and either snaffle or liverpool bits so that the trainer has considerable scope to experiment with and to use to best advantage. Some horses work better in side checks than in an overdraw style of checkrein. This is usually found by trying both and choosing the one that produces the desired effect. A noseband or caveson is not a requisite, but quite often a horse will be easier to control with one on and adjusted properly. If an overdraw checkrein is used and the trainer feels the need of one, a running martingale may be used in conjunction with a snaffle bit. A separate overcheck bit may also be employed and either straight or jointed style is allowed.

The breast collar should not be too heavy or wide; two inches is the maximum for this purpose and sewn on traces with flat style and adjustable ends are complimentary to the turnout. The neck strap should be no wider than ¾ inch and will look better if held back by a tab to the backpad hook. The backpad looks showier and tidier if the top surface is of patent leather. The bellyband should be of a comfortable width and have wrap straps. Crupper can be either sewn on or buckled on and the hardware nickel or brass. Breeching is not worn in this class. Reins are usually black with tan hand parts.

Vehicle

A two or four-wheeled vehicle is allowed in this class. If a four-wheeled buggy is your choice, a fine harness show buggy is the usual style used. However, other types of four-wheeled buggies may be used and no penalty is involved for such. There are several types of two-wheeled carts available so that you may choose one that is in proportion to your horse. Varnished wooden carts are very pretty and flatter the horse considerably, but metal carts are often lighter and easier to transport from show to show. Whatever type you choose should be clean, polished, and in sound condition. Buggies should be examined regularly for loose nuts and bolts and breaks, since transporting them around constantly is hard on them.

Training

The requirements for the Pleasure Driving Pinto class include a flatfooted walk, a slow trot, and a fast trot. The young horse has already been taught all these gaits in his basic training as followed in Chapter I, so all that should remain is to perfect his technique and give him some show ring practice. More work on the transitions may help to perfect these changes and make them smooth. The check-rein may be shortened slightly depending on the head set the horse requires. Extreme high action is not required in this class, therefore rattlers should not be used to develop this action. Boots of any type are not allowed in this class, and the accent is on pleasure and smoothness rather than brilliance and snappy action.

In this class the walk must be flatfooted; an animated, snappy walk is not the type desired. The walk should be rapid, free moving, and ground-covering as well as in a straight line. Although animation is not required, the walk should be alert and elastic—it should never deteriorate into a shuffling, wandering travesty. The horse should walk on a fairly loose rein, not pulling or having constantly to be checked, but at the same time not off the bit to the point of no control. A good walk is an absolute necessity in a good pleasure horse.

The slow trot is an easy and comfortable gait; one that the horse can keep up for a long period of time without tiring. It should be done in an alert and keen manner. The horse should look as though he's interested and enjoying his work, but not pull on the reins or have to be steered constantly. He should trot in a straight line with an even cadence, moving off his hocks with free shoulder movement in front. His head should have a good elevation and set and he should carry a good tail. The slow trot must never be allowed to become strung out. The driver must keep the horse pulled together and slightly collected to avoid this unsightly condition which often occurs when a horse jogs without coordination or impulsion.

The fast trot is an elegant gait wherein the horse produces good impulsion behind and an airy, free stride in front. This trot should not be too fast (extreme speed will be penalized), but is much faster than the slow trot. The fast trot must be square, more collected, and have even and pronounced cadence. The gait must be balanced, especially on the corners, and the head carriage should be higher and prouder. At this fast trot the horse will take more hold of the reins so that greater support will have to be given to him to assist in balancing and showing to the best of his ability. Even at this speed the horse must look like a pleasure to drive and should not be pulling extra hard nor fighting the bit. He must not break gait and will need the driver's support especially on the corners to prevent this from happening.

In the lineup the pleasure driving horse must stand quietly and back up readily and easily when requested to do so. Using the pull and release system, the driver should have no difficulty in this respect since the colt has had his lessons on this subject in his basic schooling and should have perfected the maneuver. Headers are not allowed in the Pleasure Driving class so the horse must stand squarely and alone.

Pleasure Driving Pinto horse. "Candytez," P-16837, 2A97346. Pinto Arabian gelding Champion owned and driven by Virginia Walker, Surrey, British Columbia.

Roadster Class

Pinto Roadsters are to be shown to a bike at a jog trot, road gait, and then at speed. The class is judged on performance, speed, quality, and manners.

In this class the drivers must wear colors—a jacket and cap normally designed with their stable colors (usually made of silk). It makes for a very colorful class and assists the spectator in keeping track of his or her favorite. In this class the drivers must wear their entry numbers on their back rather than pinned to the cart.

Pintos in the Roadster class must be shown with full natural manes and tails; roached manes and tails are not allowed. Braiding is allowed, and Roadsters usually wear one braid in their forelock and one just behind the bridle path. Ribbons, of several colors are usually braided into the hair and often match the colors of the driver. No other type of braiding is permissible.

Quarter boots or unlined rubber bell boots are permitted in Roadster classes. These give more action to the front legs as well as affording considerable protection.

In this class the horses enter the ring at the jog trot in a clockwise direction, show at the road gait, then are reversed and show at the jog trot, road gait, and then at speed. This is the only class where the horses are required to show first in a clockwise direction of the ring.

Harness

Roadster Pintos wear a very light and elegant harness. The bridle must have square blinkers, overdraw checkrein, and should have box loop cheeks. The bit must be a snaffle, either jointed or straight, and the checkrein bit may be either but a straight bit is preferred. It is usual for the blinkers and browband to be of patent leather. A caveson or noseband is a desirable addition to the bridle because it gives more control and prevents the mouth from opening. The breast collar should be narrow and fine, no wider than 1½ inches, with sewn on traces, of flat or beaded style and slotted ends. A full running martingale is worn by Roadsters and should pass through a tab on the front center of the breast collar. The breast collar of a Roadster is usually of fancier folded and sewn type. The backpad is very fine, about 2¼ inches, and has patent leather right around. The bellyband is of the folded and sewn style with wrap straps. Shaft loops are of open style and crupper is sewn on to the fine crupper strap. Breeching is not worn when hitched to a bike. Reins can be either all russett or black fronts with tan handparts. Hardware should be solid brass if available or a good quality nickel.

Vehicle

Roadsters are shown to a two-wheeled sulky called a bike. It is a very lightweight vehicle which weighs no more than 50 pounds. In it the driver sits over the axle on a small seat with his feet up in "stirrups" mounted on the inside of each shaft. Bikes are made of wood, metal, or a combination of both. Wheels are heavy duty type to stand the rigors of fast cornering. They are usually about 26 inches in diameter and of pneumatic style. Wheels are mounted in forks to give them more support and strength.

Training

The young colt, our Roadster prospect, has already learned to trot at varying speeds obediently and has acquired balance, muscle, and a steady head carriage. Now we must train for utmost speed while maintaining form, balance, cadence, and style. We begin by raising his checkrein a hole or two, and will likely put on either bell boots or quarter boots at this time. A bit of knee action on our Roadster is desirable. The boots will aid us in this direction as well as giving some protection in case of overreaching or interference when trotting at speed. Speed cannot be attained all at once, therefore our colt must be gradually asked for more and more speed but only if he is able to maintain his form and balance while so doing. Initially you should ask for speed on the straights and take back on the corners, giving the colt support around the turns. When you send him on in the straights, take hold of him to make sure he goes right up into his bridle and works off his hind end. He must really use his hocks if he is to produce the speed and action needed in the Roadster class.

If possible, a better place to train a Roadster is out on a country road or a half-mile track where the colt can trot right on and not have to turn corners constantly. In this kind of situation he can develop his form and speed without having to worry about keeping his balance in the turns, side reining, or creating problems for his driver. Side reining is a by-product of speed and must be dealt with almost before it happens. Side reining occurs when a horse starts to turn his head to the outside of a corner to keep his balance, leads with his shoulder, and falls in with his quarters. Soon he is cutting his corners terribly and the situation grows worse rapidly. He should not be allowed to develop this bad habit. Half halts on the inside rein as he turns the corner and good support will encourage him to look and lean into his turns. The result will be balance. Once a horse has the proper balance at all speeds, he no longer needs to side rein or turn his head to the outside. However, the longer he is allowed to go on with this bad habit, the longer it takes to correct it. Out on the road or on a long track, the colt may be asked to trot on at various speeds using the proper amount of collection and control. Without the worry of cornering he can concentrate on learning how to trot at speed and will soon be able to trot right out with great form and balance. He must trot with his chin set and his legs under him. While the driver should support the horse well with the reins, this does not mean that the horse should pull or be hard-mouthed. On the contrary, the horse should be under easy control at all times and able to be brought to a walk or jog at will and with ease.

When the colt is able to trot at speed he should be trained in the ring so that cornering may be perfected. Initially, the corners should be taken slower than the straights. However, he should be taught to come out of his corners fast and with form. Practice driving right into the corners at less than top speed, then send him on hard out of the turn, supporting him especially well on the inside rein. If he ever breaks or shows any inclination to rack or pace on his corners, pull him up right away and speak to him sharply. What you say isn't as important as the tone of voice—any animal is quick to recognize and understand a chastising tone of voice. You want that colt to know he has done wrong and is not to do it again. Sometimes breaks are the fault of the driver and you must be very careful not to chastise a colt for a mistake that *you* have made! If you drop the reins slightly on a fast corner he is quite likely to break from the sudden lack of support on his mouth. That is *your* fault. Often, these breaks are caused by a poorly adjusted checkrein so that some experimenting has to be done to achieve the proper height for the best performance.

The jog trot is a medium speed gait; ground-covering, but not fast. It should be displayed with some animation and great freedom of movement. It should be just slightly collected with the horse's head set nicely and have a good steady cadence. The horse should display an alert and keen attitude while looking interested in his work.

Since the road gait is a faster speed, the horse should show good form with more animation, balance, and ability to work well in the turns. Roadsters must go well into their turns without side reining or breaking their gait, and should come out very fast in good form with true action. Their manners and mouths should be such that they can be taken up in the straights or at any time without severe bitting or obvious force. The stride should be ground-covering, easy, and look effortless. His cadence should be even and he should move with powerful diagonals. He should go pleasingly high and airy in front and must work well off his hocks.

At speed the roadster must show good form while trotting as fast as possible. He must not be sprawly-gaited in front or strung out behind, nor should he go too wide behind. He must show balance, coordination, and tremendous ability. Any tendency to pace or rack on the turns will be severely penalized in a Roadster class—their trot must be true all the time. The Roadster must stand in line quietly and back readily when asked. Headers are not allowed and drivers must remain in their carts with the horse's head checked up (except for a workout during which the horses remaining in the middle may be unchecked).

12
P.O.A. (PONY OF THE AMERICAS)

The first P.O.A. was born in 1954, the foal of an Appaloosa mare by a Shetland stallion, and was named Black Hand #1. This was the beginning of the P.O.A. registry, a registry that has grown to vast numbers since that time.

Since that beginning the breed has been refined and improved. Today the breed standard calls for a conformation between that of the Quarter horse and the Arabian horse with Appaloosa coloring and characteristics. At maturity the P.O.A. must have a minimum height of 46 inches and the maximum height must not exceed 54 inches at the withers.

The P.O.A. was developed as a pony for youngsters and their families and as such, disposition ranks very highly. The pony must be tractable enough to be trained and handled by a youngster. Size is also important, thus the rigid standards for height in the P.O.A. registry.

Developed originally as a Western Using Pony for youth, the breed has become very versatile and is now shown english, jumping, and in harness with equally good results and ability. Their gait is another of their important features; it must be smooth, easygoing, and ground-covering. There should be none of the high, snappy action such as exhibited by the Hackney or Shetland breeds. The P.O.A. should travel with his head in a comfortable upright position and go with prompt free motion which must be straight and true at all times. His form must be balanced, of good cadence, and he should carry his hocks closely. He should be easily controlled and willing.

P.O.A.'s are usually shown with roached or pulled manes. If the latter is shown the length should not exceed 5 inches. The tail should be pulled so the tip of it is even or a bit higher with the top of his hocks.

There are six basic P.O.A. color patterns:—(Reference 4)
1. *Snowflake Pattern*—basic dark body color with "snowflake" type white spots over all or part of body.

2. *Frost Pattern*—basic dark body color with "frost" type white "sprinkled" over all or part of body.

3. *Blanket Pattern*—basic dark body color with white "blanket" over croup, hindquarters, loins, back (or part of these).

4. *Leopard Pattern*—basic white body color with dark spots over entire body and neck.

5. *White with Black Spots on Hindquarters*—basic body color white with dark spots over hindquarters, loin, croup, back (or part of these).

6. *Marbleized Roan Pattern*—basic roan body color (including neck). A mixture of light and dark hairs with light color predominant and with "varnish" marks.

The maximum height of stockings on the legs of a P.O.A. is the top of the knees or hocks.

The driving classes offered for P.O.A.'s are Pleasure Driving, youth or adult; and Roadster, youth or adult.

Vehicle

The vehicle is optional for Pleasure driving, and can be two or four-wheeled. A two-wheeled cart is preferable in most cases because it is easier to handle and much less prone to accidents than a four-wheeler. The pony is shown at a flatfooted walk, slow trot, and fast trot. He must stand quietly in the lineup and back readily when requested. He is judged on manners, quality, and performance—in that order. Ponies may be shown barefoot or with light shoes. High action, extreme speed, or any tendency to prance or show lack of control is considered a fault. The pony should look and go as if he is a pleasure to drive. Set tails, gingering, or extreme over-checking are not permitted.

Harness

The harness worn in this class may be of any type as long as it is sound, in good condition, and adjusted properly. A fancy harness with large amounts of patent leather is completely unnecessary and indeed would look out of place in this class. A plain, clean, properly fitted harness— one suitable for the cart being used is all that is necessary. Some experimenting will be necessary to discover which type of checkrein and bit will work best for your pony and at what height it works to best advantage.

Training

The training the pony has already received (see Chapter I) will be all that is needed to have your pony ready to show in a Pleasure Class. He will likely need a few shows "under his belt" to settle down to the excitement and stress felt in the show ring, but mainly he will just need lots of driving—a task that is a pleasure to both pony and driver!

In Roadster classes, the vehicle should be a two-wheeled bike or road cart. The pony is shown at a jog trot, road gait, and then at speed—the same as any other Roadster class. However, he is judged on manners, performance, speed, and quality. The emphasis is on manners first!

The harness worn can be of any type for this breed, but if the driver has access to a proper Roadster harness (such as that described for Roadsters in chapter 2 under "Equipment") he would be correct to use it.

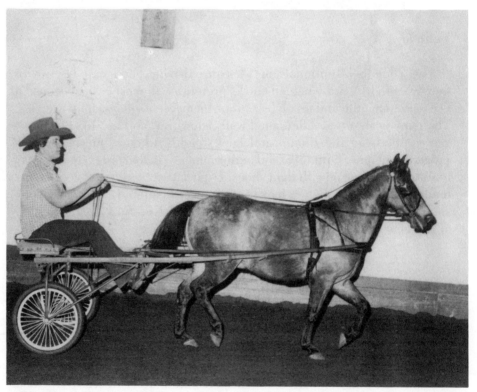

Pleasure Driving P.O.A. pony. "Tonka's Toma Hawk," #12818 owned and driven by Kim Toot, Cottage Grove, Oregon. High point P.O.A. 1974 and 1975.

The training for the various gaits is very similar to that described in chapter 2 under "Roadster" and the reader is advised to refer to these pages for the information required.

13
THE SHETLAND PONY

The Shetland pony, originating in the Shetland Islands about 200 miles north of Scotland, is one of the oldest equine breeds. There are two distinct types of Shetland ponies: the true Shetland, a small copy of a draft horse, and the more delicate and refined type with higher head, slimmer lines, and high snappy action. The latter is usually called the American Shetland. The official maximum height for a registered Shetland is 46 inches in the United States, 44 inches in Canada, and 42 inches in England.

Shetland conformation should be that of a strong, attractive, versatile pony, blending the original Shetland type with refinement and quality that results from the American selective breeding.

Shetland harness ponies are shown to a four-wheeled show buggy, usually a miniature viceroy, at a park pace and smart trot. Shetland Roadsters are shown to a miniature two-wheeled bike with the driver wearing stable colors. They are shown at a jog trot, road gait, and then at speed.

Harness classes for Shetlands include: single, maiden, novice, limit, open and ladies, amateur and junior. Then there is pair, tandem, roadster, pony fancy turnout, combination pony, junior pleasure driving, and child's Shetland pony turnout. With all these classes it is no wonder these little fellows have become so numerous and so popular.

Equipment

For all single harness classes except Roadster, the harness worn is as follows: The bridle should be a fine showy type with side checks, round blinkers and usually a liverpool bit. Browband, blinkers, face drop, and noseband should usually be patent leather and the browband often has a brass chain type ornamentation. The breast collar should be narrow and

156

fine, of folded and sewn type with patent leather overlay, and usually has buckled on traces. The backpad should be fine and fancy with much patent leather, french style shaft loops, and folded bellyband. Crupper will be the buckled on type as a tail brace is usually worn in Shetland harness classes. Hardware should be brass. Martingales, breeching or boots are not permitted. Ponies are shown to a small viceroy buggy at a park pace and "show your pony" which designates a smart trot.

At the park pace the pony should show good all around action with the feet lifted well off the ground. The stride should be free, elastic, and true (straight) and the head should be high and well set. The pony should not appear to be pulling and any roaring or choking down should be considered undesirable. At "show your pony" the Shetland should exhibit a good straight diagonal gait with the forelegs raised at least to a point where the forearm is extended in a horizontal position with the elbow and the hocks flexed. The feet should be well under the body and well off the ground. The pony should be well-balanced, have good cadence, lots of animation, and brilliance. Speed is not required or desired and excessive speed will be penalized.

In ladies, amateur and junior classes, manners are paramount and the ponies must remain checked while lined up. They must back readily at the judge's request. In all other single classes, the ponies may be unchecked at times while lined up and are not usually required to back. Another regulation concerning ladies, amateur, and junior classes is that the pony is to be shown only at the park pace and must be bitted and driven in the half cheek. Stallions are not permitted in ladies or childrens harness classes.

The harness worn in Roadster classes is quite different from that in which the harness ponies are shown. The bridle must have square blinkers, overdraw type of checkrein, and a snaffle bit—either straight or jointed. The breast collar should be very fine and have sewn on traces. (Buckled on traces are quite acceptable but not as strong or reliable.) Thimbles and a running martingale are always worn in a Roadster class. The backpad should be fine and trimmed with patent leather, and a leather housing is usually worn under the saddle. The crupper should be the sewn on flat type. Tail braces are not allowed in Roadster classes. Hardware should be brass. Boots are permitted and are usually worn both for protection and to promote higher action. Ponies are hitched to a Roadster cart, a small two-wheeled bike. They enter the ring in a clockwise direction at the jog trot and show at road gait. They are then reversed and shown at jog trot, road gait, and finally at speed. In this class drivers must wear their numbers on their backs rather than on the cart or buggy. The drivers also wear "colors" in the Roadster class. This includes a jacket and cap of matching color combinations, usually their stable colors.

At all speeds a pony should work in form; that is, with chins set and legs working beneath them, going collectedly and in form. The jog trot is a medium speed gait, ground-covering but not fast. It should show animation and a great freedom of movement. It should also be collected, with the pony's head set and working well off his hind quarters. At the road gait the speed is increased considerably. The pony must maintain his form while displaying great animation, balance, and the ability to work in the turns. There must be no side reining or breaking gait in the corners. The pony must go into his corners flat and come out fast and true. He should display good Roadster action, look brilliant, and have show ring presence. When asked to drive on the pony should make a fast neat transition to full speed while retaining form. His cadence should remain true and his headset steady as he speeds around the ring. His balance must be perfect in the corners; he must not pace or mix his gaits or become strung out behind. Ponies should be shown on the rail at all times, passing only when absolutely necessary. They should be light of rein, easily controlled and appear capable of being taken up at any time. When lined up, Roadsters must stand quietly checked up and without headers.

For Shetland pairs and tandems the equipment is the same as that described in chapter 5 for Hackney ponies.

In the Pony Fancy Turnout class, ponies enter the ring to the right at a park pace. They are shown both ways of the ring and must always be driven at a safe speed. This class is to be driven by a boy accompanied by a girl, both 14 years of age or younger. Only mares or geldings may be used. In this class the buggy—a viceroy—usually has a hoop fastened to it which supports the girl's dress. The class is judged 50 percent on the childrens' attire, 40 percent on conformation, manners, and performance of the pony, and 10 percent on neatness and cleanliness of the harness and vehicle. In the lineup ponies are required to stand checked and a header is allowed. Ponies are not required to back.

The harness worn in this class is usually the same as that worn in the single harness pony classes—a very fine quality harness.

The Junior Pleasure Driving Class is for children under 18 years of age. Only mares or geldings may be shown in this class and they must be hitched to a two or four-wheeled vehicle other than a viceroy. In this class the Shetland is shown at a walk and trot, and must be bitted with a snaffle or in the cheek position. When lined up the pony must stand quietly and back readily.

The pony must be shown with a keg shoe or barefoot; no pads or weight are permitted. Excessive speed and extreme action will be penalized in this class where the emphasis is on pleasure type.

At the walk the pony should display a flat, free easy stride, neither doggy nor prancy. His trot should be a pleasure trot—a ground-covering, free moving gait, showing willingness, obedience, and easy control. His ears should be alert and forward and he should move on easily without either continuous urging or constant pulling up.

The harness used in the Pleasure class should match the vehicle used. A two-wheeled pleasure cart or a light four-wheeled buggy will only require a light show harness, such as described for single harness Shetlands but with less fancy trimmings and patent leather on it. If the vehicle is heavier, a wider breast collar should be used to permit the pony to pull the load in an easier manner.

The Child's Shetland Pony Turnout must be driven unaccompanied by a child under 14 years of age. The pony is shown at a walk and a trot, and must stand quietly and back easily. The emphasis in this class is on the suitability, manners, and training of the pony for the purpose of being a child's pony. He should go easily and willingly, ears alert, light-mouthed and easily controlled, and must stand quietly while lined up *without* a header. Attendants are not allowed in the ring in this class. The pony must be driven in the half cheek position of the bit and be shown to a two-wheeled vehicle suitable for a child. No race or Roadster carts are permitted.

This is an appointment class and the following items (appointments) must be carried in the vehicle: blanket, water pail, halter, halter shank, body brush, curry comb, hoof pick, umbrella, raincoat, and rubbers. No other appointments are permitted. These appointments should be neatly packed and arranged in a safe manner in the vehicle where they will be handy if needed.

The harness worn in the Child's Shetland Pony Turnout should be of a pleasure type show harness, rather than a normal fine harness style. The vehicle will likely be heavier than a viceroy so will require a wider, stronger breast collar. If it is very heavy will also require breeching. Backpad, blinkers, and browband should be trimmed with patent leather and side checks and a liverpool bit should be worn on the bridle. Nickel hardware will be adequate but brass is much showier. The two-wheeled cart may be of various makes and made of either metal or wood. It should,

Shetland Pony Fine Harness. "Jumpin Jupiter," owned by Marvin Kehler, Aldergrove, British Columbia.

Shetland Pony Phaeton Class. "Edition's Top Award L." Owned by Marvin Kehler, Aldergrove, B.C. and driven by Val Kehler with Mark Kehler as escort.

Shetland Pony Fancy Turnout. "Editions Top Award L." Owned by Marvin Kehler, Aldergrove, B.C. and driven by Mark Kehler escorting Rhonda Reitsama.

Shetland Pony Roadster. "Tamberlane's Golden Rose," owned by Marvin Kehler, Aldergrove, B.C. and driven by Tom Wells.

however, be suitable for the size and build of the pony. It must be a proper cart having a floor and the like, and not a sulky or bike type where the feet rest up in stirrups. It should be of a size capable of holding the necessary appointments without crowding and its design should be safe for a child to drive.

Training

The training of the harness Shetland follows the same lines as that of the Harness and Hackney Ponies (see chapter 5). The training of a Roadster is detailed in chapter 8.

14
THE WELSH PONY

The Welsh Pony, often called "The Aristocrat of all breeds", originally came from the hills and valleys of Wales. He was there even before the Romans! His survival of severe winters, sparse vegetation, and rough and mountainous terrain insured perpetuation of only the hardiest of stock. Hence the development of a pony with remarkable soundness.

During the reign of Henry VIII, the king passed a law that all horses under 15 hands were to be destroyed. Fortunately the Welsh pony escaped this massacre, largely due to the wilderness and inaccessability of the country in which he lived.

Down through the years the Welsh pony has had to adapt to many different jobs. He pulled chariots in ancient times, worked in coal mines and on ranches, and has proven himself as the ideal family pony. He is sensible, gentle, and trustworthy for a child to handle yet has the spirit and endurance to please an adult.

It is believed that the Welsh pony possesses traces of Arabian blood and in some Welsh mountain ponies Hackney blood is reputed to be responsible for the action they've developed.

Welsh ponies were imported into North America as early as 1880. Mr. George E. Brown of Aurora, Illinois, appears to have been one of the first real Welsh enthusiasts since he imported a large number of ponies between 1884 and 1910. He called the Welsh "the grandest little horse yet produced."

Welsh ponies can be any color except piebald or skewbald. They have small, clean-cut heads with bold eyes, small ears, and a tapered muzzle. They should have a lengthy neck, long sloping shoulder, short strong back, well coupled loins, and fine hind quarters with tail set on high and carried gaily. Their action should be quick, free, and straight from the shoulder, with well flexed powerful hocks.

Welsh ponies are shown in two distinct categories: Section A—12:2

hands and under, and Section B—over 12:2 hands but not exceeding 14:2 hands.

Classes for Welsh ponies are many and varied. In pleasure driving, formal driving, and fine harness the classes are: open, maiden, novice, junior, ladies, amateur, pairs and tandems. In the Roadster driving pony the classes are: open, maiden, novice, junior, ladies and amateur.

Pleasure Driving Ponies

In the Pleasure Driving classes, the ponies must be shown with a natural foot and unweighted shoes. Even pads are prohibited. The foot must not be longer than 4 inches for section A ponies or 4½ inches for Section B ponies. The shoes, including pads, must not weigh more than 12 ounces for either section. Section A ponies must wear unbraided manes while braiding is optional for Section B ponies. Except for the Fine Harness section, Welsh ponies may not wear spoon cruppers or show evidence of a gingered or set tail. If such is found the pony will be disqualified.

Equipment

For all Pleasure Driving classes the pony will wear a light, fine, showy harness. Type of bridle is optional, i.e., the pony can wear round or square blinkers, snaffle or a liverpool bit, overdraw checkrein or side checkrein. Convention dictates however that round blinkers are usually used with side checks. A snaffle bit goes well with either round or square blinkers and an overdraw checkrein. If using an overdraw checkrein a running martingale should be used. A noseband or caveson is a good idea with either type of bridle. It serves not only to keep the pony's mouth closed but to secure the cheek pieces of the bridle in place. The latter is very important as a safety measure. If the cheek pieces slip back bringing the blinkers with them, the pony can see to the rear and may take fright and run off with disastrous results.

The breast collar should be fine and just wide enough to suit the vehicle being used. Sewn on traces are usually the type recommended since they are stronger and easier to procure than the buckled on style. The backpad should be fine, well-shaped, and a proper size for the pony. The bellyband with wrap straps should be soft and pliable and the crupper should be sewn onto the crupper strap. Reins are usually black with tan handparts but are equally correct in all russett leather. Patent leather dresses up the harness and is usually found on the blinkers, browband,

and backpad of a Pleasure Driving harness. Hardware looks better if it is brass, but nickel may be used with no disadvantage. Breeching is not worn in the show ring unless a heavy vehicle is being pulled, such as in a costume or old-fashioned class.

In Pleasure Driving classes ponies are shown in two or four-wheeled vehicles, but viceroys, racing sulkies, or Fine harness buggies are not allowed. Usually the ponies show in light two-wheeled carts of wood or metal construction. Ponies are shown at a walk and trot. They must stand quietly in line and back readily. (Tandem classes are not required to back.) The class is judged on manners, performance, style, breed type, and conformation—in that order.

At the walk, the Welsh pony should exhibit a true walk with no jigging or hitching. It must be flatfooted, fast, elastic, and showy. It should never be dull, lazy, stumbly, or dragging. The pony should walk alertly and willingly and look like he is really going somewhere. He should go kindly without pulling hard or showing difficulty in control.

At the trot he should move out freely with quick, square action and straight from the shoulder well away in front. A good reach is very important. His hocks should be well-flexed and drive powerfully under the body. He should move straight with his hind feet and hocks as he reaches forward. He should carry a proud head, a gay tail, and show alert keen interest in his work. He should look like a pleasure to drive and handle easily with light rein. Extreme speed is not desirable and will be penalized.

For pair and tandem harness see chapter 5, "Hackney Pairs" and "Hackney Tandems." Welsh ponies can wear this same harness and be considered correct. They may also wear bridles with square blinkers, overdraw checkreins, and snaffle bits.

Training

Welsh Pleasure Driving ponies require little training beyond that level of competence already acquired in chapter 1. They have learned to walk and trot properly, stand in line quietly, and back up willingly. All they need now is to become accustomed to the noise and excitement of the show ring and this they can only obtain from experience in a real show. Some experimenting will have to be done to find the best height for the checkrein to produce both the head carriage and free light motion desired in a Pleasure Driving pony. After three or four shows the pony should be settled down and ready to carry on his show career. Any special problems

Welsh Pony Pleasure Driving. "Bambi Three R." Section A Welsh. Owned by Pat Clay, Strathmore, Alberta, driven by Jean Loader. Shown winning at Calgary International 1975.

Welsh Pony, Pleasure Driving. "Gow's Golden Count" owned and driven by Heather McLellan, Midnapore, Alberta.

arising out of these first few show ring appearances may be worked on at home. Clapping is sometimes a problem at early shows. It excites a green pony and makes him want to move. Simulating this noise at home by having friends clap and make noises or by playing records of clapping will usually accustom the pony to this aspect of showing.

Formal Driving Ponies

Formal Driving ponies are shown with long natural manes and long, unset, ungingered tails. It is permissible to braid the forelock and the first strand of the mane behind the ears. The pony must carry a natural foot with unweighted shoes. Pads may be used in this section, but any additional weight is prohibited. Quarter boots, spoon cruppers, false tails, or evidence of gingering are all prohibited and a pony will be disqualified by their use.

In Formal Driving classes the ponies are shown at an animated natural trot and an animated walk. They are required to stand quietly in line and to back readily. The class is judged on performance, manners, style, breed type, and conformation.

The Formal Driving pony must be an upstanding individual and a real athlete. To obtain the free movement necessary in this class the pony must have a good length of forearm and a good sloping shoulder. He should be a high-couraged animal, lively, animated, and able to show brilliance at all gaits. A doggy, quiet, and lazy pony will not make a good Formal Driving prospect.

The animated natural trot is an extremely brilliant trot wherein the forefeet shoot forward and dwell an instant at full stretch with a floating movement before touching the ground (not round action). This movement is combined with hock action that is powerful and well-raised, while the hind leg is brought forward with a swinging stride. This gait demands a high degree of collection and necessitates the greatest output of energy at both ends of the pony.

The animated walk should be rapid, collected, elastic, true, and in a straight line. There must be no tendency to jig or amble and the pony must not appear sluggish or strung out. He should exhibit an eager expression, ears pricked, neck flexed and give the impression that he is actually going somewhere.

Equipment

The harness worn by the Formal Driving pony is similar to that of the Pleasure Driving pony, but is finer and shows more patent leather. The insert in the breast collar will usually be of patent leather. The panels as well as the backpad will also be patent. Formal Driving ponies usually wear overdraw checkreins, square blinkers, and snaffle bit, but other types are permissible.

The vehicle used in this class must be a four-wheeled vehicle and is usually a miniature fine harness buggy. It should be clean and gleaming, have a good paint job, and will show up better if trimmed in chrome.

Training

The training for this class naturally follows that of the Pleasure Driving pony. The pony will have shown a potential for this class and all that is required is to bring out his natural abilities and develop them into the desired pattern. Your pony has already obtained balance, cadence, and lightness from the previous training, now you must begin to collect him and ask for some animation. You will want the pony to work well off his hocks and to be light and airy in front.

Start by shortening his checkrein a hole or two to begin to shift the weight off his front end. As he trots along, cluck him on but restrict him gently with the reins. You want animation, not speed, and as he puts more effort into his work, spurred on by our encouragement, the effect will be an animated, positive action at the *same* speed. Extreme speed is undesirable and is penalized in the show ring. However, when you are first training the youngster, you will have to allow much more speed than the show ring gait in order to encourage and train him. After he has established the amount of animation desired and understands what is required of him, you can slow him down. To slow him down at first is just to frustrate him and discourage his attempts to please.

With the impulsion from the hind end and the restraining but gentle contact from the bit, a brilliant float will eventually be achieved by the front end. The pony's muscles and timing must be built up gradually to withstand and produce a high degree of animation and brilliance, so you must be careful in training not to tire the youngster unduly. Never keep a steady pull on the pony's mouth. This will only serve to make it hard. Use squeezes and gentle tugs to keep the mouth alert, soft, and responsive.

The animated walk is achieved in the same manner, i.e., by sending him on while restraining him gently. Care must be taken that he *does* walk and does not break into a jog or trot. The play on the reins must be very sensitive and subtle to achieve this showy gait and requires considerable practice.

The reverse, back up, and lineup are done in the manner already perfected in earlier work.

Fine Harness Ponies

Ponies shown in this class wear long natural manes and long, unset, ungingered tails. The forelock and first strand of the mane are usually braided with colored ribbon, and a spoon crupper or tail brace are optional. Quarter boots may also be worn in this class.

Fine Harness ponies are extremely brilliant, beautiful, and full of presence. Their long flowing manes and tails, proud head carriage, good action, and obvious enjoyment of their work make this a most thrilling class to watch. Fine Harness ponies show at a free animated park trot and an animated walk. They are required to stand quietly and to back readily. The class is judged on performance, manners, style, breed type, and conformation. Faulty or laboring action is severely penalized as is excessive speed.

The animated park trot is a very animated, elegant trot displaying considerable action wherein the pony works well off his hocks. He must have perfect balance and cadence and show a good diagonal motion. His front action must be free and flowing, never stilted, choppy, or tied in. This is where the long sloping shoulder is necessary to provide the freedom of movement.

The animated walk should be true, elastic, rapid, collected, and in a straight line. The pony must look very alert and keen but show easy control and willingness. He must never appear lazy, dull, doggy, or strung out in a Fine Harness class.

Equipment

The harness worn in this class is a very fine, light, showy harness with a great deal of patent leather trim and solid brass fittings. The pony is required to show in a snaffle bit with overdraw checkrein. Square blinkers are usually worn, and a noseband or caveson is a good idea. A running martingale is worn, the forks of which are often of rounded leather. Breast collar and backpad are very fine, narrow, and covered in patent leather. Open shaft loops are used in conjunction with wrap straps. Thimbles or breeching are not worn in this class. The crupper is usually buckled on since a tail brace is customarily used (or sometimes a spoon crupper).

Reins are either all russett or black with tan handparts and are made very fine. Handholds are undesirable because the pony is expected to have good manners and be easily controlled.

Ponies in this class are shown to a viceroy or miniature fine harness buggy.

Training

The training for the Fine Harness class follows the same lines as those described for the Formal Driving class. From his basic training he is gradually checked higher and asked for increasing animation and impulsion while being restrained gently to a proper speed. His action will be much rounder than the Formal Driving pony and will attain a greater height as well. His stride should never become trappy or choppy. He must have a good reach and this should be encouraged as he is trained. The use of quarter boots or bell boots will assist in achieving the action desired, and as these are worn in the show ring it is good practice to accustom the pony to their use. A good fit is essential both for comfort and best performance.

The pony must work well off his hocks while also displaying good hock action. He must travel straight all around. A good farrier is very important to both achieve balance and correct any faults in this area. Any tendency to wing or cross their feet at the trot must be corrected right away because this fault can develop other bad habits in their way of going.

Some experimenting will have to be done with the checkrein in order to achieve best results. It must not be too high (tight) or it will ewe the pony's neck and restrict the freedom of motion. It also must not be too low (loose) or the pony will become heavy on the forehand. He must be able to use and flex his neck to provide the balanced form so necessary to the elegance of his trot.

Once the animated park trot is established fairly well, slow your pony down to an animated walk. This can be achieved by keeping him up to the bit as he is pushed along while restraining him to a graceful tempo. Care must be taken that he hold to this gait and not quicken into the trot. A delicate, sensitive play of reins is the method by which this is achieved.

The head set of a Fine Harness pony is very important and a bitting rig may be used to advantage in achieving this quality. Care must be taken not to overdo their use and to make sure it is used in a humane manner. See chapter 2 for a complete description of a bitting rig and the various adjustments possible.

Welsh Pony Fine Harness. "Starlights Blue Sky," #14963, owned by Mr. and Mrs. R. Weide, Norco, Calif. and driven by John Enirich of Walnut Creek.

Roadster Pony

Welsh Roadster ponies must be 50 inches or under. Ponies must wear long natural mane and long, unset, ungingered tail. The forelock and first strand of the mane behind the ear may be braided. Quarter boots are permitted and are usually worn.

The requirements for this class are the same as all Roadster classes and the training follows the same lines. The reader is invited to read the section on "Roadsters" in chapter 2—the Arabian Horse. The order of consideration in judging this Roadster class differs for the Welsh. It is judged on performance, manners, style, and speed in form and breed type.

Welsh Pony Roadster. "Chamcook Coch Brightboy" #1228, Welsh Pony stallion owned and driven by Mr. Martin Renner of Surrey, B.C. This fine pony has never been out of the ribbons in fifteen years of showing.

15
PREPARING FOR A HORSE SHOW

Getting ready for a horse show is hectic at the best of times, but if you have a system and follow it consistently you will find it a lot simpler. It will still be a great deal of work but you will be working most efficiently and accomplishing the necessities in a definite order.

Clipping and Trimming

The day before the show you should do all the clipping on your horse or pony. If done earlier, it will not look as neat because hair grows quickly and can look untidy very quickly.

Clipping is usually done with the horse on cross-ties to keep him in one place. Clip his bridle path around the forelock and both around the edges of his ears and the insides of his ears. This is a touchy part of horses and must be done with patience and some skill. Packing the ear with a big wad of cotton wool will be of some help because it keeps the hairs from falling down in his ear and cuts down the sound of the clippers. Small size clippers are best for this job as they fit in small places easier and also are much quieter than the big Clipmaster size. Clip all the hairs off around his muzzle and chin and the eyelashes around his eyes. Clip tight up under his jaws to give the appearance of a nice clean jaw line. Next clip around the fetlocks, pasterns, and the long hair around the coronet bands. The feet and lower legs look 100 percent better for this, especially if the animal has white stockings.

Pull the mane and tail to achieve the type of effect you desire or that is required by his breed type.

Hoof Cleaning

The hoofs must be washed thoroughly and all dirt and stains removed

173

either with a stiff brush or sandpaper. If they are white hoofs, they should look white, not manure-stained or dirt streaked, (These stains are often difficult to remove.) This job is best started a few days before the show so that by the day of the show you have achieved a clean, smooth hoof surface.

The day before the show you can put on the first coat of hoof dressing, which will preserve the clean finish you have achieved and make it easier to touch up the day of the show. Use a clear hoof dressing on the white feet, and "hoof black" on black or dark feet. These come in small cans with a dobber to apply the liquid. The job is best done with the horse on cross-ties on a clean, dry, hard surface. Leave him standing there until the hoofs are completely dry.

Bathing

The day before the show is usually bath day for the horses if the weather is warm enough to permit it being done without worry of catching cold. There are many shampoos on the market for washing horses and special ones for washing the manes and tails. If you don't have these special items, you can give a very adequate bath with just warm water. Make sure you scrape the horse down quickly afterwards and put on a wool cooler to prevent a chill. Human hair shampoo works well on manes and tails, but make sure you rinse thoroughly to get all traces of shampoo out of their skin. Ordinary hand soap does a good job on white stockings. Again, be sure to rinse it all out when you are finished.

The day of the show you may wish to enhance the whiteness of the stockings on your horse. Cornstarch powder rubbed into the white hair, then brushed out does a good job, but the author prefers "dog chalk," a preparation sold at pet stores which comes in a convenient round block and is easier to apply than the cornstarch. Either one will give that final "finish" to your horse's grooming.

Braiding

Braiding has to be done the day of the show in order to look neat and tidy. However, it should be taken out immediately after the show to prevent the hairs from being pulled out.

Harness ponies are braided with three pieces of colored ribbon fastened together at one end. One braid is put in the forelock and one braid in the first strand of the mane behind the ears. A small amount of hair is used to anchor the braid and is braided in with the ribbon. A flat braid is used and both ends of the ribbon are snipped in a "V" shape after the braid is tied and finished. The length is optional but is usually left about eight inches below the length of the mane.

Hackney ponies are braided very differently from that described above for Harness ponies. The Hackney is braided the entire length of his mane in small braids tied with colored yarn. Usually about twenty-two tiny braids are put into the Hackney's mane and one in his forelock. The mane is pulled to a length of about 4 inches to facilitate braiding and the forelock is clipped off entirely except for a tiny strand—just enough for one braid. The yarn used is usually rug yarn weight and can be any color although red, green, and blue seems to be the ones used most frequently. The yard should be pre-cut into lengths of about 18" to speed up the braiding process. This is something you can do days before the show. A braiding box is a handy item in a show trunk. It is a small box that holds the yarn, scissors, comb, and sponge. This way *all* the braiding equipment is in one convenient box and ready for use when needed.

To braid the mane, wet it slightly with the sponge, part it into about ¾—1 inch widths of mane and begin the braid. After about 2" of braiding start the yarn—folded in two—and braid it into the hair, finishing off by tying two half-hitches at the end. For best results braid the entire mane before tying the braids up into the finished "knots" along the top of his neck.

To tie the braids, double up the braid at the neck end and have it stick up about one inch. When that is done, tie it around itself and end by tying the yarn into a secure knot plus a double bow. The double bow is to provide more yarn for color when the yarn is cut. Tie all the braids, making certain the line is straight down the top of the neck. Now, using the scissors, cut off all the bows of yarn about ¼ inch from the braid all the way up the mane evenly. This type of braiding is very neat, eye-catching, and is also one of the trademarks of the Hackney.

Allow yourself a good hour for the braiding part of your show preparation. A stool to stand on of whatever height you prefer will make it a much easier task to braid the mane. With practice you will likely cut down the braiding time considerably.

Once the pony (or horse) is braided, leave him on cross-ties until the class is called, otherwise he may lie down and roll or somehow manage to mess up or rub out his braids.

Cleaning the Harness

The harness must be thoroughly cleaned and polished before the show.

Take it completely apart and clean it with a good glycerine preparation (or your favorite leather cleaner). Dry it thoroughly and apply a coat of harness dressing if the leather looks dull. The patent leather benefits by a small amount of vaseline rubbed well in and then buffed to a high shine.

Clean the brass either with a liquid brass cleaner or the more practical wadding that is now available. Shine it with a soft cloth and it should really gleam.

Reassemble the harness, making sure it goes back into the same holes as before (providing it was properly adjusted for your horse to start with!). Pack the clean harness in the show trunk between the folds of a soft blanket to keep it clean and shiny. If you don't use a show trunk, put it into a harness bag and draw the drawstring up tightly to keep out the dust.

It is wise to bring some extra pieces for your harness in case of breakage, such as a checkrein, throat latch, neck strap, and checkrein tab. A package of shoe laces provides an instant repair kit for many problems. Make sure they are the right color for your horse or harness.

Grooming

The horse or pony should be well-groomed and completely ready for the class entered at least an hour early. This means his feet are picked out and the hoof dressing applied, his white sox have been chalked or corn starched, his tail has been brushed and combed (or picked strand by strand if preferred), his mane groomed or braided, his eyes and nostrils shined up with vaseline or baby oil, and his coat sprayed with Show Sheen or whatever preparation you prefer. Once ready he should be left on cross-ties to make sure he stays clean. A light sheet can be thrown over him.

Harnessing

The horse should be harnessed at least half an hour before his class and allowed to wear it in his stall on cross-ties. This is especially necessary if a tail brace or spoon crupper is being used. This period allows the horse's muscles to adjust to the tightness or fit of the harness. Also, by harnessing this early the competitor has time to make any adjustments necessary on the show harness.

While the horse stands harnessed and ready on cross-ties, you should prepare the show buggy or cart for the class. Give it a final shine and park it ready to hitch in a place that will not be hemmed in or difficult to drive out of.

Packing the Show Trunk

Packing for a show always presents a dilemma. We are worried lest we forget a vital item and often take far more than necessary or sometimes the opposite. Below is a list of essentials:

Grooming equipment	Wheel wrench for buggy or cart
Hoof dressing	Bicycle pump
Clippers and oil	Small medical kit
Braiding box	Clean towels
Show sheet or blanket	Cornstarch or chalk
Hammer, staples, nails, screw driver, pliers in a small tool kit	Baby oil or vaseline
	Wool cooler
Harness and some extra pieces for it	Extra halter and shank

In addition to your show trunk you will have to bring adequate feed for the show, buckets and feed tubs, as well as the buggy and any other accessories you decide upon. These may include lawn chairs, small tables, tack room covers, and decorations. A small mirror kept in the show trunk will prove handy.

Your clothes also must be chosen and packed. Make sure you have a complete outfit for each class. Gloves and driving apron are handiest when kept in the show trunk. In that way they are always there when needed.

A smock or coverall is also a handy item in the wardrobe for a horse show. It can be put on over your show clothes and will keep you clean while working around the horse. Make sure it is large enough to slip on and off easily over your clothes, otherwise at the last minute you may be trying frantically to wriggle out of it (and may mess your clothes in the process).

You are now ready for your class. Good luck and HAPPY DRIVING EVERYONE!

References

Captain C. Morley Knight, *Hints on Driving*. London England: J.A. Allen & Co. Ltd., 1969.

Tom Ryder, *On the Box Seat*. Macclesfield, England: Horse Drawn Carriages Ltd., 1969.

James C. Harrison, *Care and Training of the Trotter and Pacer*, Columbus, Ohio: United States Trotting Association, 1969.

Pony of the Americas Handbook. Mason City, Iowa: P.O.A., 1976.

INDEX

179